BENTO

SHIRLEY
WONG

Kawaii
かわいいお弁当
Bento

Marshall Cavendish
Cuisine

Editor: Lydia Leong
Designer: Bernard Go Kwang Meng
Photographer: Calvin Tan

Reprinted March 2015

Published by Marshall Cavendish Cuisine
An imprint of Marshall Cavendish International

Other Marshall Cavendish Offices:
Marshall Cavendish Corporation. 99 White Plains Road, Tarrytown NY 10591-9001, USA • Marshall Cavendish International (Thailand) Co Ltd. 253 Asoke, 12th Floor, Sukhumvit 21 Road, Klongtoey Nua, Wattana, Bangkok 10110, Thailand • Marshall Cavendish (Malaysia) Sdn Bhd, Times Subang, Lot 46, Subang Hi-Tech Industrial Park, Batu Tiga, 40000 Shah Alam, Selangor Darul Ehsan, Malaysia.

National Library Board, Singapore Cataloguing-in-Publication Data

Wong, Shirley.
Kawaii bento / Shirley Wong, little Miss Bento; editor, Lydia Leong; designer, Bernard Go Kwang Meng; photographer, Calvin Tan –
Singapore: Marshall Cavendish Cuisine, [2014]
pages cm
ISBN : 978-981-4561-43-3 (paperback)

1. Cooking, Japanese. 2. Bento cooking. 3. Food presentation. I. Leong, Lydia, editor. II. Go, Bernard Kwang Meng, designer. III. Tan, Calvin, photographer. IV. Title.

TX724.5.J3
641.5952 — dc23 OCN 891161088

Printed in Singapore by Colourscan Print Co. Pte. Ltd.

Dedication

This book is for my husband, Steven Low, for bearing with the mess in the kitchen after my cooking adventures.

Acknowledgements

I would like to thank my family and husband for their never-failing encouragement. Without them, this book would never have been completed.

I am also grateful for the support I received from the team at Marshall Cavendish. To my editor, Lydia Leong, and designer, Bernard Go, for their patience and advice, and the photographer, Calvin Tan, for making my bento creations look amazing in the photographs. Thank you for bearing with the long hours for the photography session, often without taking meal breaks.

Throughout my bento journey, I have also received overwhelming support from readers who follow me online. This has given me the motivation and determination to continue with this journey. Thank you.

I would also like to thank those whom I have not yet met, but who are just as crazy about bento-making and cooking. Thank you for picking up this book.

Contents

Introduction 8

What is Bento? 10

Bento Tools & Equipment 12

Typical Bento Ingredients 18

Basic Bento Techniques 20
- Cooking Japanese Rice 20
- Shaping Rice Balls (Onigiri) 21
- Wrapping Rice Balls with Seaweed 22
- Creating Different Expressions 23
- Securing the Parts Using Pasta Sticks 23
- Colouring Rice 24
- Colouring Hard-boiled Quail Eggs 25
- Making Egg Sheets of Different Colours 26
- Egg Sheet Colour Chart 27
- Shaping Characters Using Mashed Potatoes 28
- Tracing and Cutting Characters 29
- Using Seaweed and Oblate Sheets 30
- Putting Together a Character Bento 32

Bento Recipes
- Weather Themed Bentos 35
- Seasons Themed Bentos 45
- Special Occasion Bentos 55
- Festival & Celebration Bentos 65
- Animal & Nature Themed Bentos 77
- Fairy Tale Themed Bentos 95

Bento Decorative Items 106

Character Templates 112

Stockists 115

Weights & Measures 116

Introduction

When I started sharing my bento creations online, I also started getting requests for bento tutorials and advice. As the number of requests grew, I began toying with the idea of writing a cookbook to share basic bento techniques and bento design ideas.

This book, which you now hold in your hands, is the culmination of my years of interactions with those who visit my blog, attend my cooking classes and/or other bento-making events. It will give you a good background on the basic bento techniques essential for putting together cute bentos, known in Japanese as *kyarabens*.

Once you are familiar with the basic bento techniques, the possibilities are endless! Feel free to modify the designs and substitute ingredients as you wish, according to your preference and taste and/or what is available.

You will also notice that I have included bentos using different staples, from rice, to noodles and bread, as bentos are not limited to rice. Bentos can be put together using any ingredient that meets your specific dietary preferences or needs, so go ahead and experiment!

I hope you will enjoy using this book as much as I had fun creating these original bento recipes and designs for you.

Happy bento-making!

Shirley Wong
Little Miss Bento

What is Bento?

Bento simply means lunchbox in Japanese. Putting together bento boxes and enjoying bento meals are integral parts of everyday life in Japan where children bring home-made bento to school for lunch, and adults similarly bring home-made bento or purchase bentos for their meals. With the globalisation of food cultures, bento-making has found its way into different countries, and is now also popular here in Singapore.

This growing interest in making bentos and especially character bentos, is spurred on by parents who want to ensure that their children eat healthy meals, so *kawaii* (or cute) character bentos are the answer not just to healthy meals, but meals which will appeal to children as well. Others see character bento-making as an extension of their cooking skills, or they simply enjoy creating cute characters in their bento (also known as *kyaraben*, *charaben* or *decoben* in Japanese).

When putting together a character bento, it is important to strike a balance between creating a wholesome meal and the presentation of the bento. While presentation is important in making character bentos, the taste is just as important. Bento is afterall a meal to be eaten and enjoyed. This is something I strongly believe in.

If you are a beginner in character bento-making, try not to be overly ambitious. Do not incorporate too many elements in your bento, but focus on a key item as your main design and leave time to prepare the side dishes for the bento. These side dishes will make the meal complete.

It is also advisable to plan the design of your character bento and the side dishes beforehand. I usually sketch out my designs the night before, and sometimes even days ahead. This approach guides me as I plan the ingredients, and makes the bento-making process more efficient. This means saving precious time on cooking while making the whole experience thoroughly enjoyable.

Bento Tools & Equipment

A wide array of bento boxes and bento tools are available online or from bento or bakeware stores. The following pages highlight some useful tools to have on hand.

Bento Cutting Knives and Precise Cutting Knives

These are great for cutting ingredients, and are essential when making intricate designs using seaweed.

Bento Picks

Bento picks can be simple or feature different themes and characters. Use them to skewer ingredients such as edamame beans, fruits and meatballs. They make excellent decorations and help highlight the theme of your bento.

Branding Iron

These handcrafted iron presses were originally used for decorating traditional Japanese sweets (*wagashi*). However, they are now also popularly used to create prints on Japanese egg rolls (*tamagoyaki*), pancakes, bread and even cookies.

Cling Wrap

Cling wrap is extremely convenient for shaping rice balls. It makes freehand moulding clean and easy, so you don't have to wet your hands to prevent the rice from sticking to your hands. Wrapping the rice balls in cling wrap also helps prevent the rice from drying out while you work on the other parts of the bento.

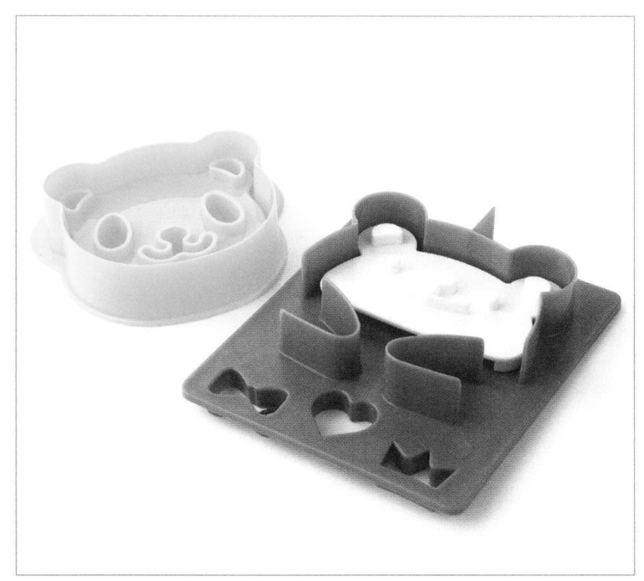

Cutters

Cutters are one of the most useful tools for making character bentos as they are available in various shapes that would be difficult to cut freehand, and are great time-savers. Metal cutters are durable and are perfect for cutting harder and thicker ingredients. Sandwich cutters are great for making fun shaped sandwiches for bread-based bentos. Browse bento stores and bakeware stores to find various cutters.

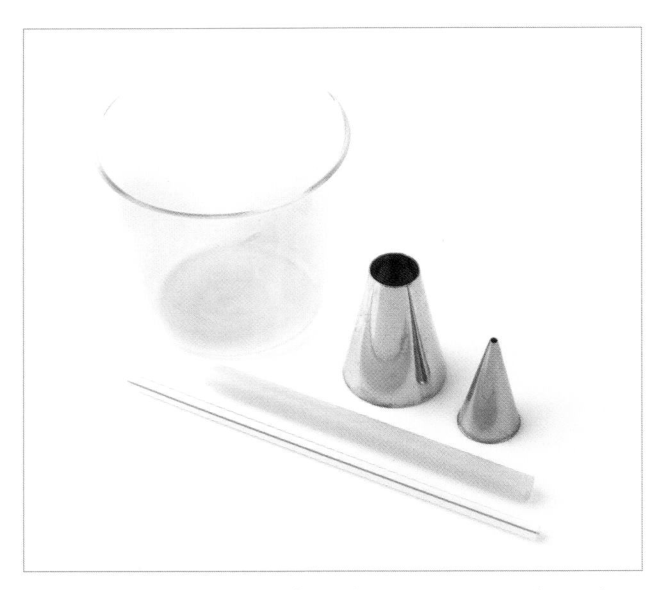

Everyday Household/Kitchen Items and Tools

Get creative! There are many everyday items and cookware that can double up as cutters or tools in bento-making. These include drinking straws, piping tips and cups etc.

Food Cups and Containers

Food cups and containers are great for keeping the different ingredients and side dishes in your bento separate. Use them to hold ingredients and/or sauces that may stain your bento box. Do take note of the different quality of these containers however, as some are microwave-safe, while others are not.

Onigiri Moulds

Onigiri moulds help make moulding rice into different shapes easy. They are useful for beginners, and are also a time-saver when preparing a large number of bentos, since they ensure consistency in the shape and size of the rice balls. Wet the moulds before filling with rice so the rice can be easily removed after shaping.

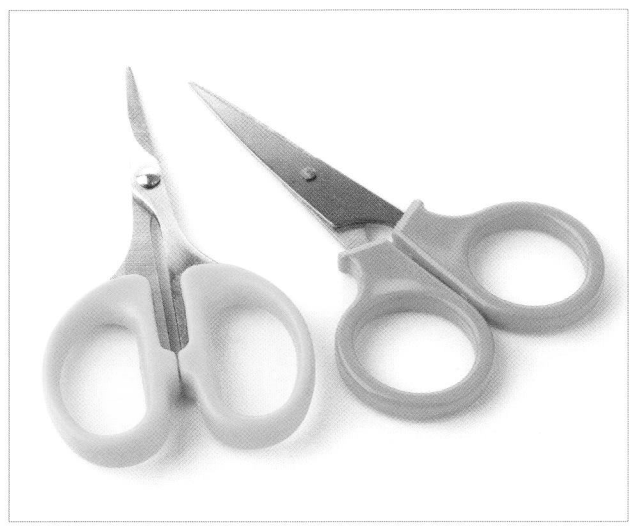

Scissors

A pair of small, sharp scissors will play a huge role in the cutting of small decorative parts and details for character bentos.

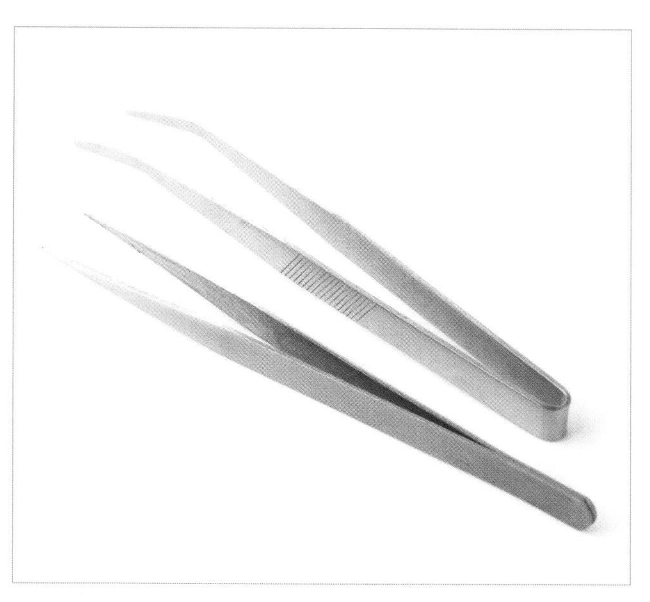

Tweezers

Tweezers facilitate the handling and adjustment of small details in your bento.

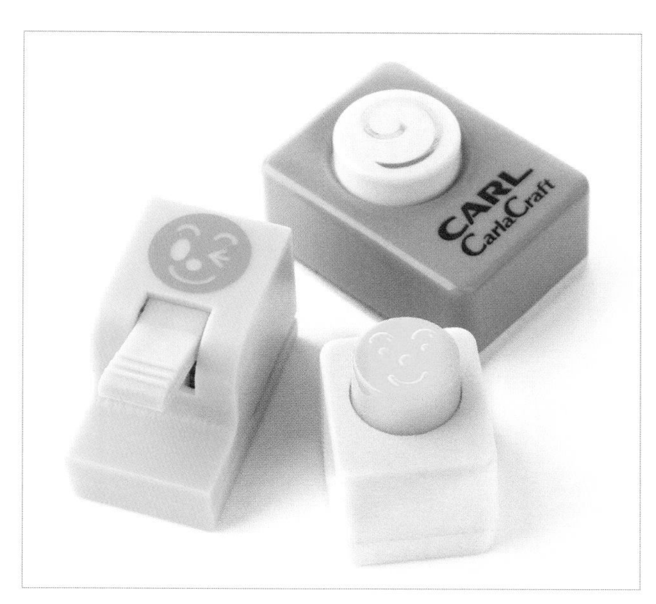

Seaweed (Nori) Punch

These are specialised punchers designed for cutting fine facial features from seaweed. The paper punchers from craft stores can also be used in a smiliar way. While using scissors gives you more control over the desired size and shape of the seaweed cut-outs, the seaweed punchers make it possible for really fine parts to be created with ease.

Wax Paper

Wax paper is excellent for lining wooden bento boxes to ensure that sauces and/or oils from the food are not in direct contact with the wood to prevent staining. This is especially useful when using traditional bent wood (*magewappa*) bento boxes. Wax paper comes in a variety of designs, and you can match them to the theme of your character bento. Decorative wax paper is available in limited designs in locals stores. A wider variety is available online.

Bento Boxes

Bento boxes are available made from different materials and in a variety of shapes and sizes. This includes traditional bent wood boxes (*magewappa*), microwave-safe boxes, aluminium boxes, thermal containers and disposable boxes. Choose a bento box based on your needs, as well as your budget. For example, does the food require reheating? If so, a microwaveable box would be ideal. Does the food come with a lot of sauce? If so, a box with a sealed lid would be useful.

Your meal serving requirements will also affect your choice of bento box. The volume of the bento box (in millilitres [ml] or cubic centimetres [cc]) is usually indicated on the product specifications. Here is a general guide:

- Children — 350 ml/cc to 500 ml/cc
- Women — 500 ml/cc to 800 ml/cc
- Men — 800 ml/cc to 1200 ml/cc
- Family/Group — above 1200 ml/cc

Furoshiki

Furoshiki is a type of traditional Japanese wrapping cloth that can be used for wrapping and carrying bento boxes. They are available in a variety of attractive prints. A *furoshiki* of at least 50 x 50-cm is necessary for a regular size bento box.

Typical Bento Ingredients

There is no limit to what you can add to your bento, and here are some typical ingredients I use for character bentos. They are available from some local supermarkets and Japanese supermarkets, or online.

Crabsticks (*Kani Kamaboko*)

Japanese Fish Cake (*Hanpen*)

Pink Japanese Fish Roll (*Kamaboko*)

Seaweed (Nori)

Sliced Cheese

Fried Tofu Pockets (*Aburaage*)

Commercial Egg Sheets (*Usuyaki Tamago*)

Oblate Edible Sheets

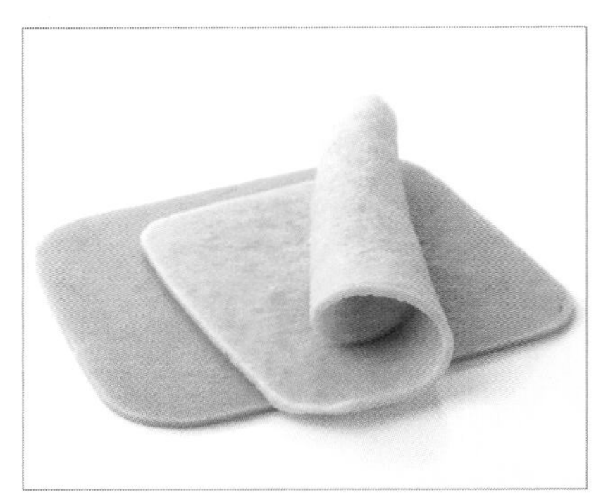

Sliced Ham

Mini Sausages

Bonito Flakes (*Katsuobushi*)

Pink Fish Floss
(*Sakura Denbu*)

Multicolour Rice Crackers
(*Arare*)

Character Pasta
and Pasta Shapes

Spaghetti, Somen and Udon

Sushi Seasoning Mix

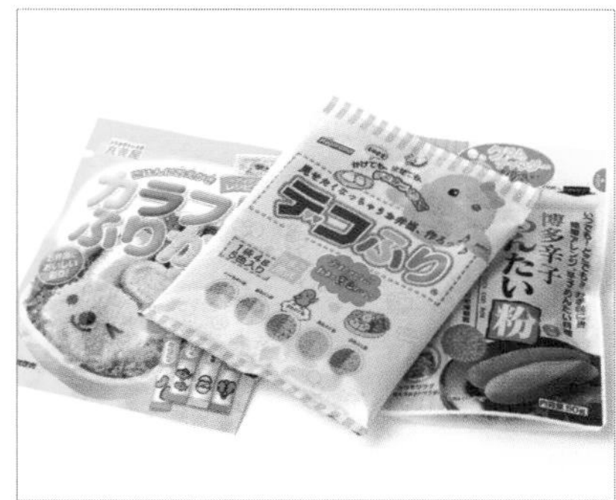

Deco Rice Topping
(Deco *Furikake*)

Character Rice Topping
(Character *Furikake*)

Basic Bento Techniques

COOKING JAPANESE RICE

Ingredients

1 cup Japanese rice

Water, as needed for rinsing rice

$1^1/_3$–$1^1/_2$ cups mineral water to cook rice (You can also refer to the markings indicated in the Japanese rice cooker.)

NOTE Normal drinking water can be used to cook the rice, but using mineral water will make the cooked rice more fluffy and have a beautiful gleam.

Method

Rinse the rice about three times. Do not rub the rice grains, but use your hand to swirl the water gently. Drain.

Add the mineral water to the rice and let soak for at least 30 minutes.

Cook the rice in a rice cooker according to the manufacturer's instructions.

When the rice is done, let rest for about 10 minutes in the rice cooker. This will allow the rice to absorb the residual heat and cook more evenly. The grains will also be firm and not mushy.

SHAPING RICE BALLS (ONIGIRI)

Place the rice in the centre of a sheet of cling wrap. Leave it plain, or add a filling if desired. Bring the ends of the cling wrap together, then twist and tighten the ends, while shaping the rice into a compact ball. Mould it to the desired shape.

Shaping a plain rice ball

Shaping a rice ball with filling

WRAPPING RICE BALLS WITH SEAWEED

When wrapping seaweed around a rice ball, the trick is to cut slits along the edges of the seaweed to ensure that the seaweed wraps around the rice snugly. Then, wrap the rice ball back in the cling wrap and let rest.

CREATING DIFFERENT EXPRESSIONS

The expressions of your characters play a huge part in the final look of your bento. Get creative and try out various designs to create different looks!

NOTE Placing the eyes lower, closer to the mouth, can help create a cuter look.

SECURING THE PARTS USING PASTA STICKS

Fine pasta sticks can be used to secure some details to the character, while at the same time preventing them from shifting when the bento box is moved or transported.

NOTE The raw pasta sticks will absorb moisture from the other ingredients in the bento and soften after some time. They can then be consumed safely. Alternatively, deep-fry the pasta sticks until golden brown before using, if preferred.

COLOURING RICE

There are many ways to make your bento colourful.
The table below offers some suggestions. Be creative!

Red	Ketchup	Marinated Fish Roe (*Mentaiko*)	Red Rice Topping (Red *Furikake*)		
Pink	Pink Rice Topping (Pink *Furikake*)	Salmon Flakes	Pink Fish Floss (*Sakura Denbu*)	Pink Sushi Mix	
Yellow	Yellow Rice Topping (Yellow *Furikake*)	Mashed Hard-boiled Egg Yolk	Japanese Egg *Soboro*		
Orange	Orange Rice Topping (Orange *Furikake*)	Boiled Shredded Carrot	Prawn Roe (*Ebikko*)		
Green	Green Rice Topping (Green *Furikake*)	Boiled and Mashed Edamame Beans			
Brown	Japanese Light Soy Sauce	Teriyaki Sauce	Cooked Minced Meat	Corned Beef	Bonito Flakes (*Katsuobushi*)
Purple	Purple Rice Topping (Purple *Furikake*)	Dried Red Perilla Mix (*Yukari*)	Chopped Purple Cabbage		
Blue	Blue Rice Topping (Blue *Furikake*)				
Black	Black Sesame Powder				

COLOURING HARD-BOILED QUAIL EGGS

Coloured hard-boiled quail eggs are useful for making cute characters and designs for your bento. Hard-boiled quail eggs can be coloured using ingredients such as curry powder (yellow) and Japanese light soy sauce (brown) or food colouring.

Method

Place the quail eggs in a saucepan half-filled with water. Bring to the boil and cook for 6–7 minutes.

Remove the hard-boiled eggs and peel.

While the eggs are still warm, place them in the colouring solution and let soak until the desired colour is achieved.

NOTE When soaking the eggs in soy sauce, they will float due to the salt content (see inset picture, top right corner). As such, you will need to rotate the eggs at regular intervals for the colour to be even. You can skip this step if just one side of the egg will be visible in your bento. You can also use the different colours in your design, such with the owl in the Graduation Day bento (page 62).

MAKING EGG SHEETS OF DIFFERENT COLOURS

Ingredients

Eggs or egg whites (See chart)

1/2 tsp cornflour, mixed with 1–1 1/2 tsp water (for egg whites)

A little food colouring (optional)

NOTE The coloured egg mixture will lighten slightly when cooked, so take note when adjusting the desired colour tones.

Cook the egg over very low heat to reduce bubbling and burning. This will ensure that the egg sheet is smooth.

Method

Beat the eggs or egg whites lightly.

If using egg whites, mix the cornflour with some water and add the food colouring, if using. Mix well.Add to the beaten egg whites.

Strain the egg/egg white mixture to remove any air bubbles. Use a fine sieve for egg whites.

Lightly oil a frying pan. Add the egg/egg white mixture to form a thin layer. Cover pan and cook over low heat.

When the egg sheet is about 80% done, turn off the heat and let the egg sheet sit for 20–30 seconds to finish cooking in the residual heat.

Remove from the pan, being careful not to tear the egg sheet. Use as desired.

Making a yellow egg sheet using whole eggs

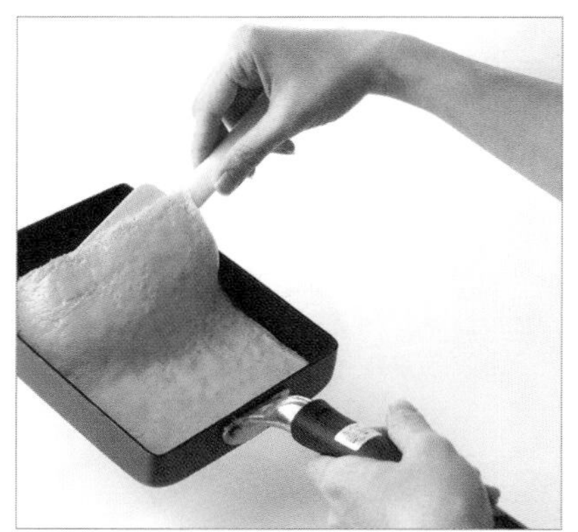

Making a coloured egg sheet using egg whites and food colouring

EGG SHEET COLOUR CHART

These measurements are for a regular size egg pan. Adjust as needed according to your pan size.

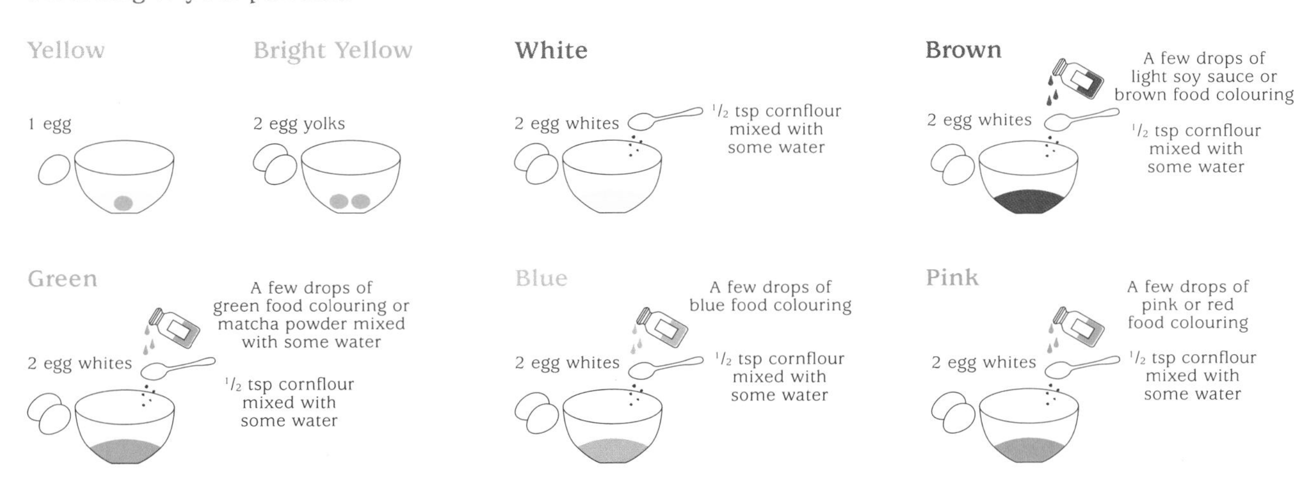

SHAPING CHARACTERS USING MASHED POTATOES

Besides rice, character bentos can also be made using mashed potato. Choose smooth and creamy potatoes such as Japanese or russet potatoes. Colour can be added using food colouring. Knead until the mashed potato is evenly coloured. Shape the mashed potato as you would dough. Assemble the parts to create the character.

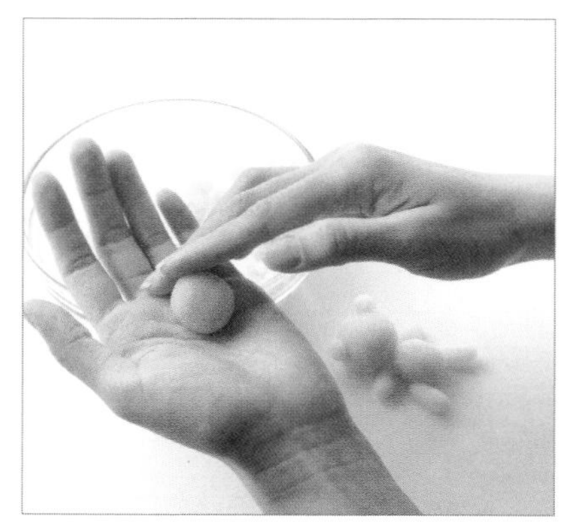

TRACING AND CUTTING CHARACTERS

Once you have identified an image for your bento character, trace it out using baking paper. Visualise the different layers required and trace the respective sections. Cut out the sections and lay them on the ingredients. Use a cutting knife to cut along the outline. Assemble the layers to complete the design. (Character templates, page 112–114.)

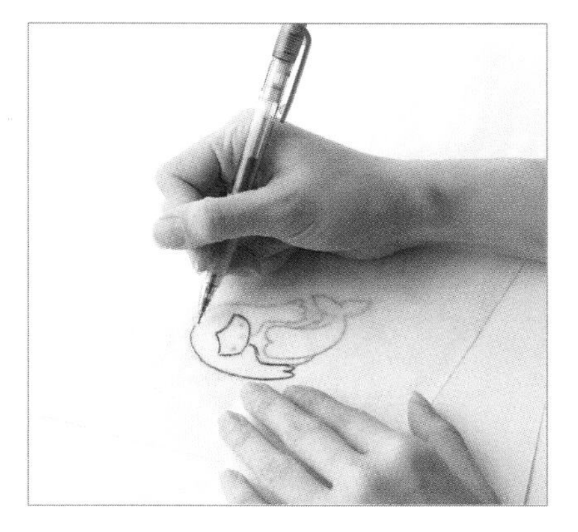

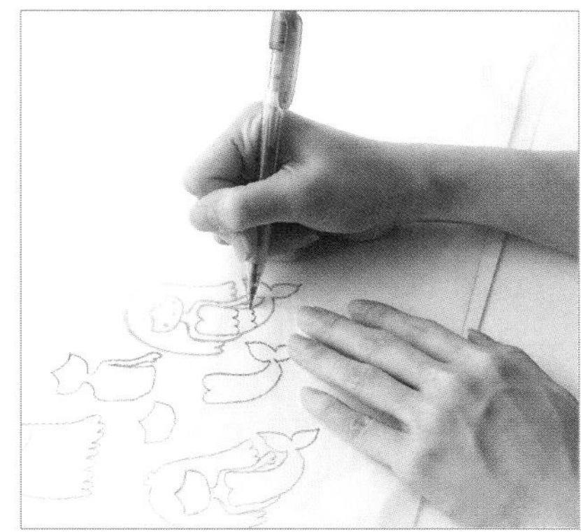

USING SEAWEED AND OBLATE SHEETS

Detailed designs can be done using seaweed and oblate sheets.
The panda character template used here is available on page 114.

Ingredients

1 seaweed sheet

1 oblate sheet

NOTE Cut the design from the inside out, starting with the smaller parts.

When wetting the oblate sheet, do not drag the cloth over the sheet or it may 'melt' or tear.

Method

Place one sheet of the design over the seaweed on a cutting board. Hold in place using clips. Cut the design using a precise cutting knife. Set the seaweed cutting aside.

Place the oblate sheet on a transparent board with the other copy of the design below. Dab the oblate sheet using a moist lint-free cloth. The oblate sheet will become sticky. Gently tap with your fingers to check that you have sufficiently moistened the neccesary area.

Place the seaweed cutting on the oblate sheet using the design below as a guide. Use a tweezer to place the finer parts more accurately. Set aside to dry, the oblate sheet should no longer feel sticky.

Dilute some food colouring and colour the oblate sheet using a small fine-tipped brush if desired. If unsure, test the colour on a sheet of paper or on the sides of the oblate sheet.

Set the sheet aside to dry completely. Trim off the excess oblate sheet. Lay the design on rice or cheese in your bento.

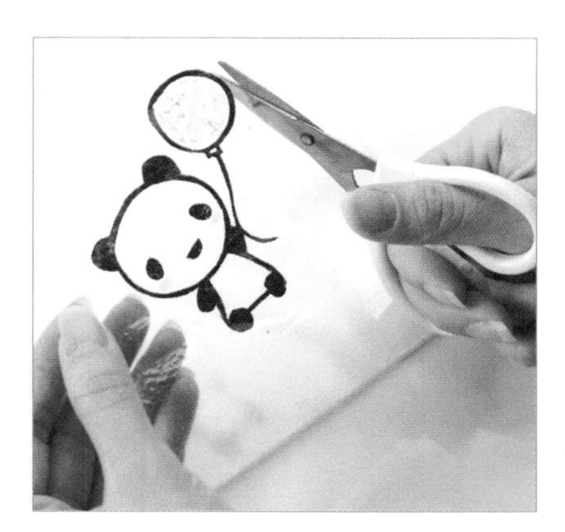

PUTTING TOGETHER A CHARACTER BENTO

Step 1. Colour the rice
Mix the egg *soboro* (made using a large egg, page 42) with 160 g cooked Japanese short-grain rice (page 20) until the rice is evenly coloured.

Step 2. Shape the rice
Divide the rice into 2 equal portions. Using food-grade plastic gloves or cling wrap, shape each portion of rice into a ball.

Step 3. Prepare the features
Using an oval cutter, cut out 2 ovals for the beaks from a slice of carrot. Using a pair of scissors, cut 4 circles for the eyes and 4 rounded Ws for the feet from seaweed. Overlap 2 sheets of seaweed when cutting features such as eyes so they will be identical.

Step 4. Complete the character
Place the features on the rice ball. Gently press the carrot beaks into the rice ball so they will adhere better. Complete the character by inserting red heart shape bento picks for the combs.

Step 5. Assemble the bento
Arrange some lettuce in the bento box, followed by the character rice balls. Fill in the bento box with the other side dishes. Decorate with with edamame beans skewered with bento picks.

Weather Themed Bentos

Sunny Day 36

Colourful Rainbows 38

Walking in the Rain 40

Moon & Stars 42

Sunny Day ぽかぽか太陽さんのキャラ弁

Character Bento

Cooking oil, as needed

1 large egg

1/4 seaweed sheet

A little ham

1 slice carrot

1 slice cheese

1 serving fried noodles with vegetables

Side Dish

Salad

1. Lightly oil a frying pan and place over low-medium heat. Cook the egg sunny-side up until the egg white turns opaque and is cooked. Remove egg to a plate. Using a knife, trim the edges of the fried egg to neaten it, if necessary. Set aside.
2. Using a pair of scissors, cut 2 circles for the sun's eyes and a curved line for the mouth from seaweed. Set aside.
3. Using a seaweed punch, cut the cloud's eyes and a mouth from seaweed. Set aside.
4. Using a pair of tweezers, place the seaweed eyes and mouth on the egg yolk. As the seaweed cannot be adjusted after it is placed on the egg, try to be precise when handling the parts.
5. Using a straw, cut 2 small circles for the sun's cheeks from ham. Position the ham cheeks on the egg yolk.
6. Using a knife, cut about 8 small triangles from the carrot to create sun rays. Set aside.
7. Using a toothpick, cut 2 clouds out of the sliced cheese. Place the cloud's eyes and mouth on one cloud.
8. Place the fried noodles in the bento box. Assemble the sun and clouds on the fried noodles. Arrange the triangular carrot sun rays on the egg white.
9. Complete the bento meal with a salad.

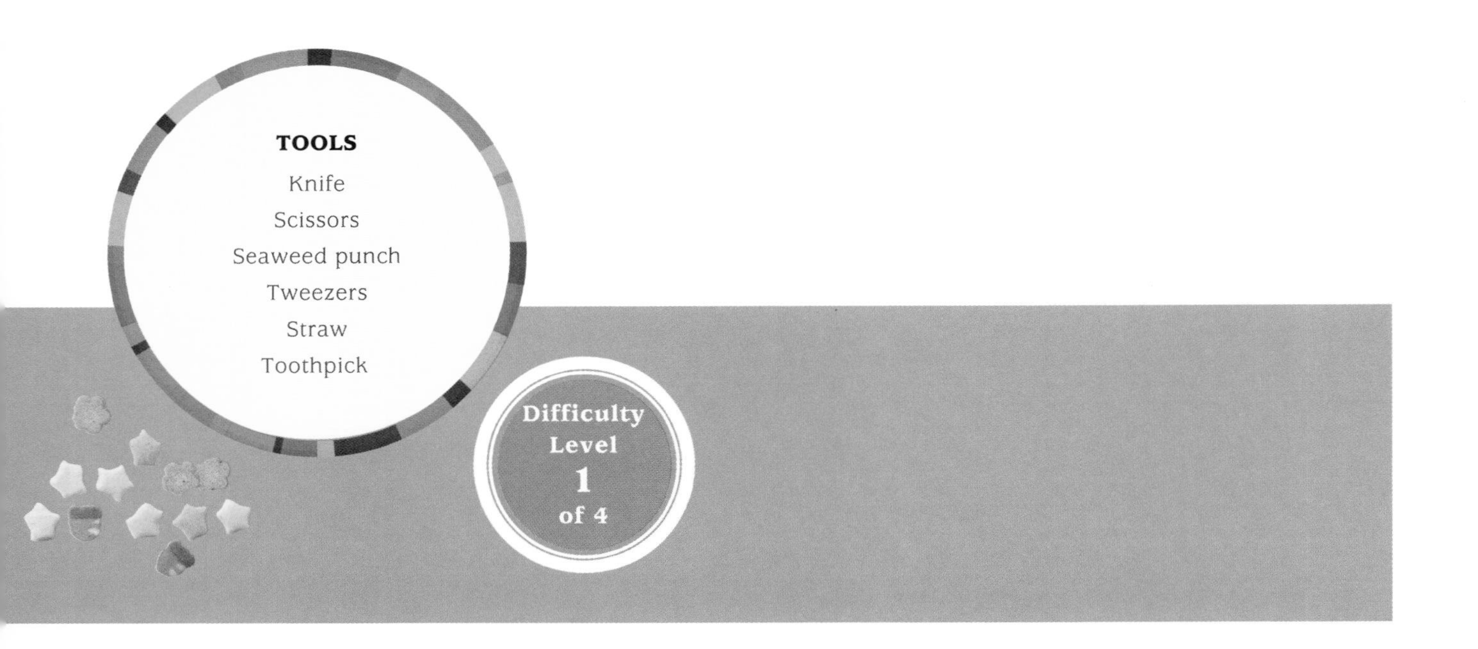

Colourful Rainbows カラフルレインボーのキャラ弁

Character Bento

1/2 red, yellow and green capsicums, cored and seeded

1 slice cheese

1/4 seaweed sheet

3 slices sandwich bread

2 strawberries, washed and hulled

1 tsp strawberry jam

1 hard-boiled egg, peeled

2 tsp mayonnaise

Salt and pepper to taste

1 1/2 Tbsp shredded carrot

5–6 slices Japanese cucumber

1 1/2 Tbsp shredded purple cabbage

1 tsp blueberry jam

Butter (optional)

Side Dish

Vegetables of choice

1. Using a round cutter or knife, cut 2 curved strips from each capsicum for the rainbows. Set aside.
2. Using a cloud cutter or a straw that has been halved, cut 4 clouds out of the slice of cheese. Set aside.
3. Using a seaweed punch, cut the clouds' eyes and mouth from seaweed. Using a pair of tweezers, place the features on the clouds.
4. Prepare the sandwiches. Cut the bread into 6 rectangles.
5. Slice the strawberries and mix lightly with the strawberry jam.
6. Mash the hard-boiled egg and mix with 1 tsp mayonnaise and some salt and pepper to taste.
7. Mix the shredded carrot with 1 tsp mayonnaise and some salt and pepper to taste.
8. Pat dry the Japanese cucumber.
9. Mix the shredded purple cabbage with the blueberry jam.
10. Sandwich the ingredients between the slices of bread in different layers. You can butter the bread if you like.
11. Trim and cut the sandwich to fit the bento box. Arrange the sandwich such that the rainbow colours can be seen.
12. Assemble the rainbow and clouds on the sandwich.
13. Complete the bento meal with vegetables of choice.

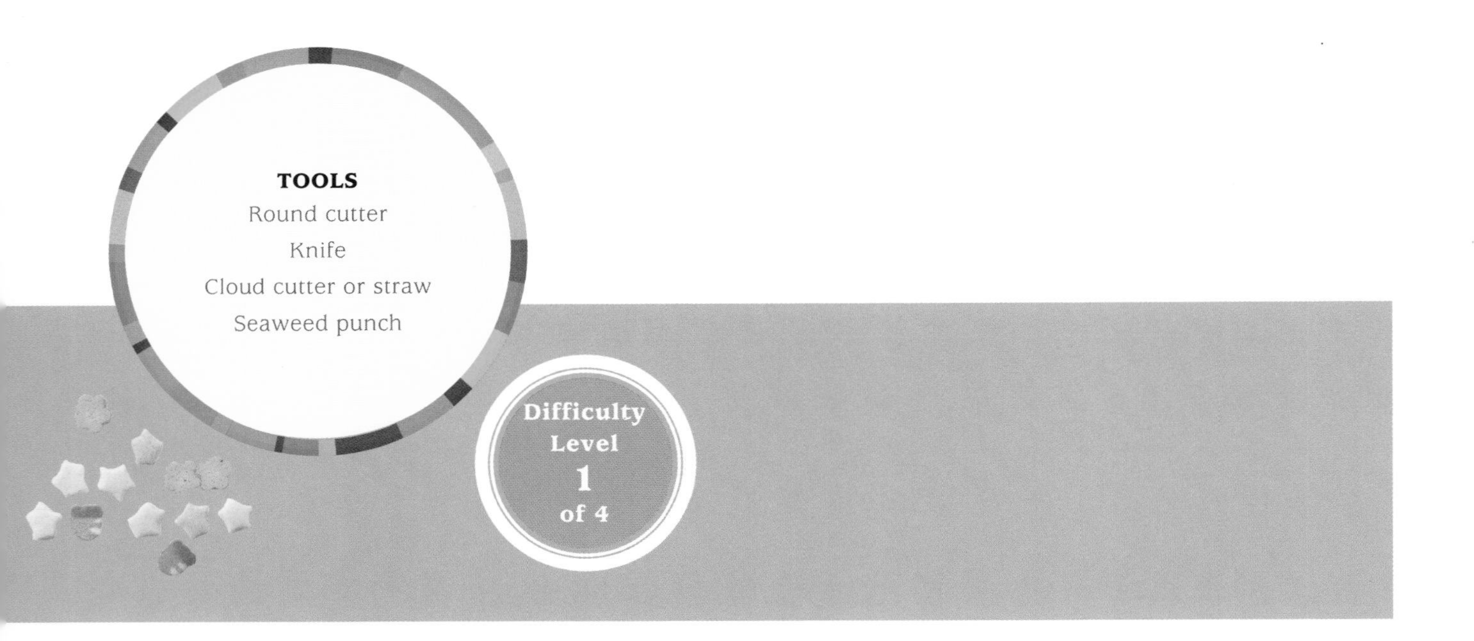

Walking in the Rain 雨の日ルンルンのキャラ弁

Character Bento

120–130 g cooked Japanese short-grain rice (page 20)

1 tsp teriyaki sauce

1 seaweed sheet

1 yellow egg sheet (page 26)

2 pasta sticks, each about 2 cm

2 red multicolour rice crackers (*arare*)

1 soba or thin udon noodle stick, boiled

1/2 slice ham

1/4 slice Japanese fish cake (*hanpen*)

Steamed broccoli florets

Side Dishes

Pan-fried meatballs

Vegetables of choice

Fresh fruit

TOOLS

Cling wrap

Scissors

Knife

Tweezers

Teardrop cutter

Bento pick with handle

Difficulty Level 3 of 4

1. Mix the rice evenly with teriyaki sauce to add colour to the girl's face. Using cling wrap, shape the rice into one large round for the girl's head and a smaller oblong for the body.
2. Using a pair of scissors, cut out a wide inverted V for the girl's fringe from one end of the sheet of seaweed, then cut the other side into a curve. Place it on the large rice ball and cut slits around the curved side of the seaweed, so it sits nicely around the rice ball for the girl's hair (page 22). Cover with cling wrap. Set aside.
3. Cut one-third off the egg sheet so it becomes a shorter rectangle. Cut the smaller piece of egg sheet into 2 short rectangular pieces and trim one end of each piece so it curves. Wrap these egg sheets around the oblong rice ball for the girl's raincoat. Secure with pasta sticks.
4. Fold the larger egg sheet and wrap it around the girl's head, being careful not to tear the egg sheet.
5. Using a pair of scissors, cut 2 circles for the eyes, 4 lines for the eyelashes and a curved line for the mouth from the remaining seaweed. Place the features on the girl's face using a pair of tweezers.
6. Place the red multicolour rice crackers on the girl's face for the cheeks.
7. Tie the soba or udon into a ribbon and place it on the girl's raincoat.
8. Using a pair of scissors, cut the ham into 2 triangles, one narrower than the other. Place the narrower piece on the wider piece to form an umbrella. Set aside.
9. Using a teardrop cutter, cut out raindrops from the fish cake.
10. Assemble the girl and umbrella in the bento box. Stick a bento pick by the umbrella for the handle. Place the broccoli in the box for the rain cloud and place the fish cake raindrops on it.
11. Complete the bento meal with side dishes such as pan-fried meatballs, vegetables of choice and fresh fruit.

Moon & Stars 月と星のキャラ弁

Character Bento

1 egg

1 tsp mirin

1/2 tsp sake

1/2 tsp Japanese light soy sauce

1/2 tsp sugar

Cooking oil, as needed

120–130 g cooked Japanese short-grain rice (page 20)

1/4 seaweed sheet

1 slice ham

3 slices carrot, boiled

Side Dishes

Meat croquettes

Sautéed vegetables and mushrooms

Salad

Fresh fruit

1. Beat the egg in a bowl. Add mirin, sake, soy sauce and sugar. Mix well. Lightly oil a frying pan and place over low-medium heat. Add the egg and keep stirring as it cooks to break up the egg into small pieces. This is Japanese egg *soboro*.
2. Mix the rice evenly with the egg *soboro*.
3. Using cling wrap, shape the rice to create a crescent. You can do this freehand or using the sides of a round container. Arrange the rice in the bento box.
4. Using a pair of scissors, cut 2 curved lines for the eye and mouth, 2 lines for the eyelashes and a swirl for the hair from seaweed.
5. Using a large straw or round cutter, cut out a circle from ham for the cheek.
6. Using a pair of tweezers, place the details on the moon.
7. Using a star cutter, cut out stars from the carrot slices. Place them in the bento box.
8. Complete the bento meal with side dishes such as meat croquettes, sautéed vegetables and mushrooms, salad and fresh fruit.

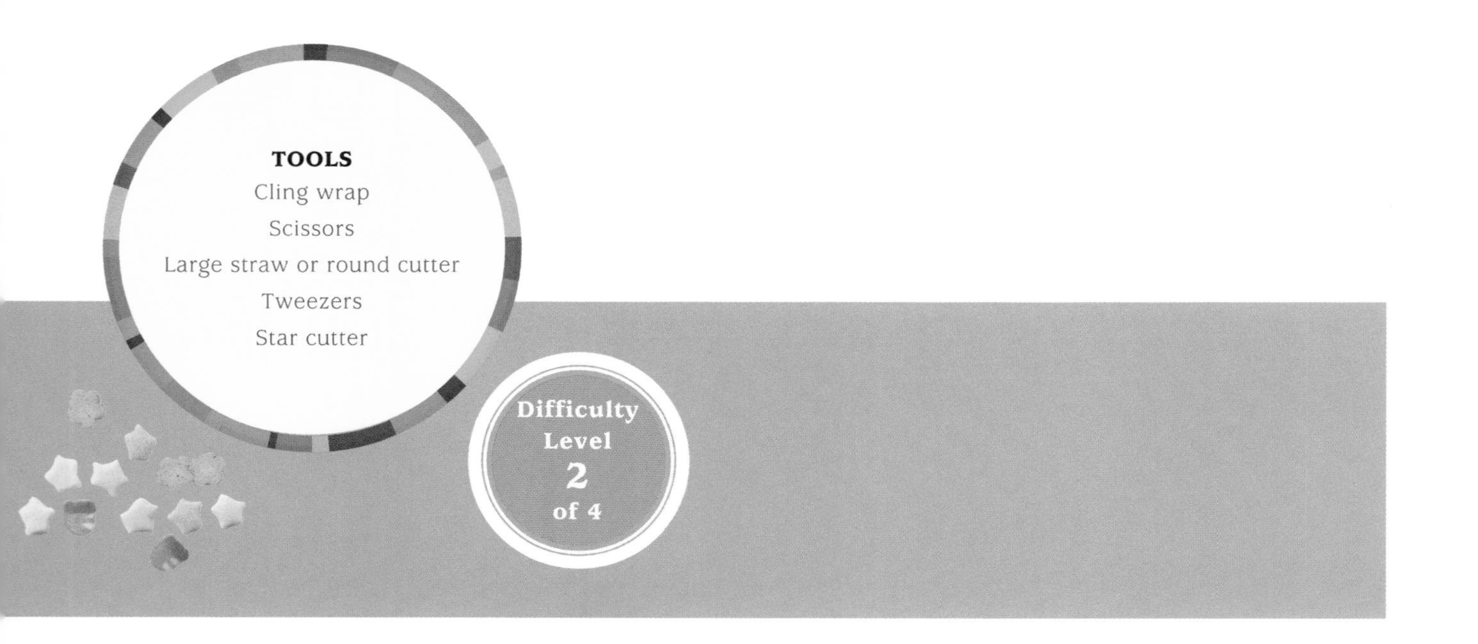

Springtime 46

Day at the Beach 48

Autumn Magic 50

Winter Wonderland 52

Springtime 春のキャラ弁

Character Bento

170–180 g cooked Japanese short-grain rice (page 20)

1 1/2–2 tsp teriyaki sauce

1 seaweed sheet

2 crabsticks (*kani kamaboko*)

1 small strip yellow egg sheet (page 26)

1 small strip green egg sheet (page 26)

1 pink soba noodle stick, boiled

1 green soba noodle stick, boiled

Lettuce

Ham sakura flowers (page 106)

Side Dishes

Grilled salmon fillet

Japanese fish roll (*kamaboko*)

Vegetables of choice

1. Mix the rice evenly with teriyaki sauce to add colour to the girl's face and body. Using cling wrap, shape the rice into one large round for the girl's head and a smaller round for the hair bun on her head.
2. Using cling wrap, shape the remaining portion of rice into an oblong shape for the body, and two small thin shapes for the arms.
3. Using a pair of scissors, cut out a wide inverted V for the girl's fringe from one end of the seaweed, then cut the other side into a curve. Place it on the large rice ball and cut slits around the curved side of the seaweed, so it sits nicely around the rice ball for the girl's hair (page 22). Cover with cling wrap. Set aside.
4. From the remaining seaweed, cut a circle large enough to wrap around the hair bun. Cut slits around the sides and wrap it around the ball. Cover with cling wrap. Set aside.
5. Using a knife, make a slit along the side of each crabstick. Peel open and tear away the red layer, leaving a thin white strip along the sides. Wrap the crabsticks around the body, overlapping them to look like a kimono.
6. Cut the yellow and green egg sheets so they are of different widths. Wrap them around the body. Loop the pink and green noodles and place over the egg sheets to complete the kimono.
7. Using a pair of scissors, cut 2 ovals for the eyes, 4 lines for the eyelashes and a curved line for the mouth from the remaining seaweed. Place the features on the girl's face using a pair of tweezers.
8. Using a flower bento pick, secure the girl's hair bun to her head.
9. Assemble the girl in the bento box with lettuce and sakura flowers. Complete the bento meal with side dishes such as grilled salmon fillet, Japanese fish roll and vegetables of choice.

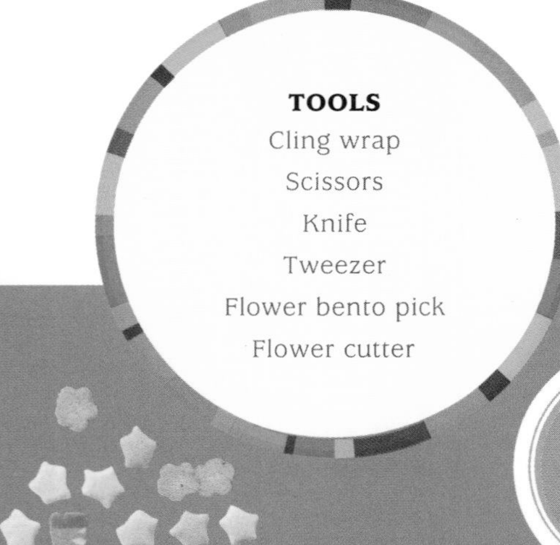

TOOLS

Cling wrap

Scissors

Knife

Tweezer

Flower bento pick

Flower cutter

Difficulty Level 2 of 4

Day at the Beach 夏のキャラ弁

Character Bento

1 small Japanese or russet potato

Sea salt to taste

$^{1}/_{4}$ seaweed sheet

1 crabstick (*kani kamaboko*)

1 round slice Japanese cucumber

3 black sesame seeds

Sausage crab (page 108)

Cucumber tortoise (page 110)

Side Dishes

2 dinner rolls

Butter, as needed

Lettuce

Grilled luncheon meat

Scrambled egg

1. Peel and rinse the potato. Cut into small cubes and steam until tender. Mash the potato and season with sea salt. Set aside until cool enough to handle with bare hands.
2. Take about 2 tsp mashed potato and shape into an oval for the bear's head. Take about $1^{1}/_{2}$ tsp mashed potato and shape into another oval for the body. Take about $^{1}/_{2}$ tsp mashed potato and shape into 2 small balls for the ears. Take about 1 tsp mashed potato and shape into 4 short lengths for the limbs. Assemble the bear.
3. Using a pair of scissors, cut 2 circles for the eyes, a smaller circle for the nose and a line for the muzzle out of seaweed.
4. Using a pair of tweezers, place the features on the bear's face.
5. Unroll the crabstick. Using a round cutter, cut a circle out of the red layer, then cut it in half. Cut the slice of cucumber in half and place the crabstick semicircle on it. Using a pair of tweezers, place 3 black sesame seeds on the crabstick to complete the mini watermelon. Position it on the bear.
6. Slice and butter the dinner rolls, Fill with lettuce, grilled luncheon meat and scrambled egg. Place into the bento box.
7. Position the bear on a dinner roll and the sausage crab and cucumber tortoise on the other bun. Decorate with seashell bento picks and a cocktail umbrella.

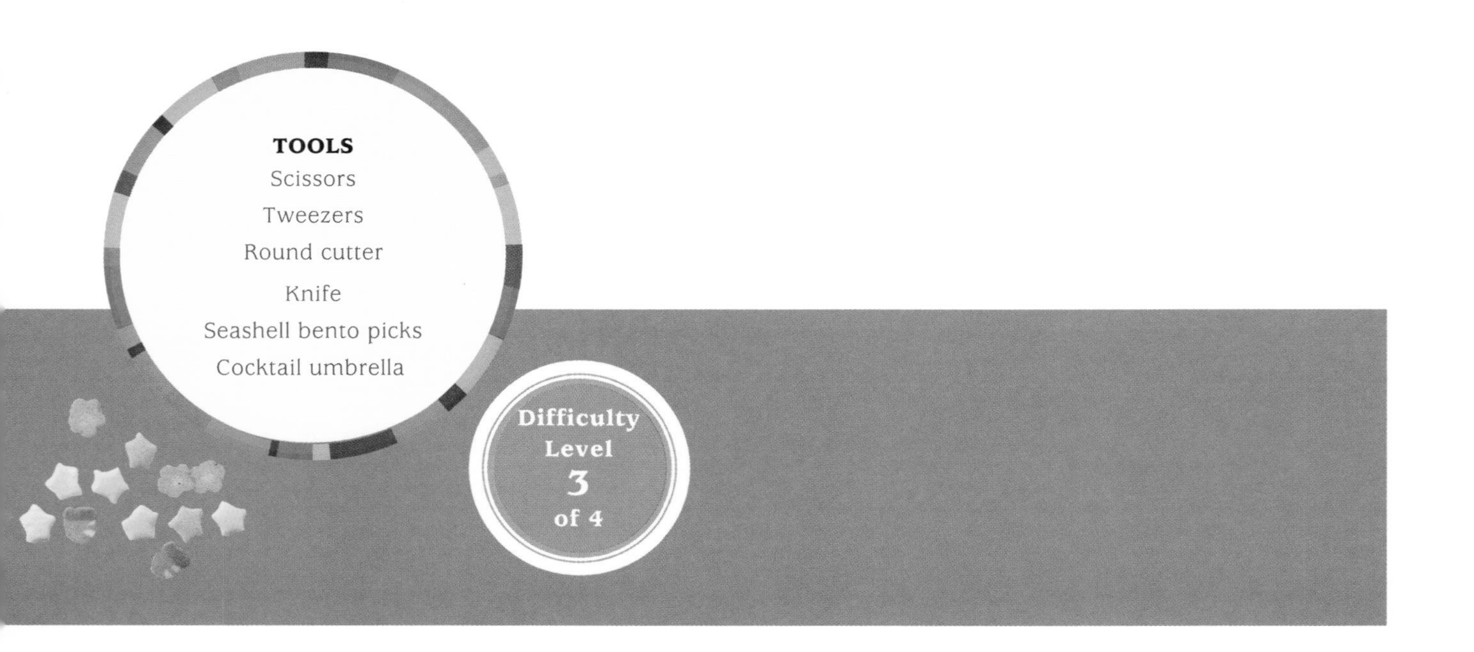

Autumn Magic 秋のキャラ弁

Character Bento

1 brown egg sheet (page 26)

$^{1}/_{2}$ yellow egg sheet (page 26)

A little ham

$^{1}/_{3}$ seaweed sheet

A little mayonnaise

150 g cooked Japanese short-grain rice (page 20)

3 sausage acorns (page 108)

1 $^{1}/_{2}$ tsp rice topping (*furikake*)

2 slices carrot, boiled

Side Dishes

$^{1}/_{2}$ Japanese cucumber, sliced

Sautéed potatoes and meat

Edamame beans

Maple mochi slices

1. Trace the drawing of the squirrel and acorn (page 112) on a sheet of baking paper. Trace the parts (ear, body, tail, tummy, centre strip of the tail, inner ears, acorn and acorn cap) separately as you will need to cut the different layers (page 29).
2. Using a pair of scissors, cut out the sections.
3. Place the ear, body and tail cut-outs on the brown egg sheet and cut using a precise cutting knife.
4. Place the tummy, centre strip of the tail and inner ear cut-outs on the yellow egg sheet and cut using a precise cutting knife.
5. Place the acorn cap cut-out on the brown egg sheet and cut using a precise cutting knife.
6. Place the acorn cut-out on some ham and cut using a precise cutting knife.
7. Using a pair of scissors, cut circles for the eyes and nose, a curved line for the mouth and lines for the squirrel's stripes from seaweed.
8. Assemble the pieces to form the squirrel. Dab a little mayonnaise on the ingredients to help secure the parts.
9. Using a leaf cutter, cut out leaves from the carrot slices.
10. Spoon the cooked rice into the bento box. Assemble the squirrel on the rice.
11. Cut the carrot slices using the maple leaf cutter.
12. Complete the bento meal with side dishes such as cucumber slices, sautéed potatoes and meat and edamame beans.
13. Decorate with the sausage acorns, carrot maple leaves, rice topping and maple mochi slices.

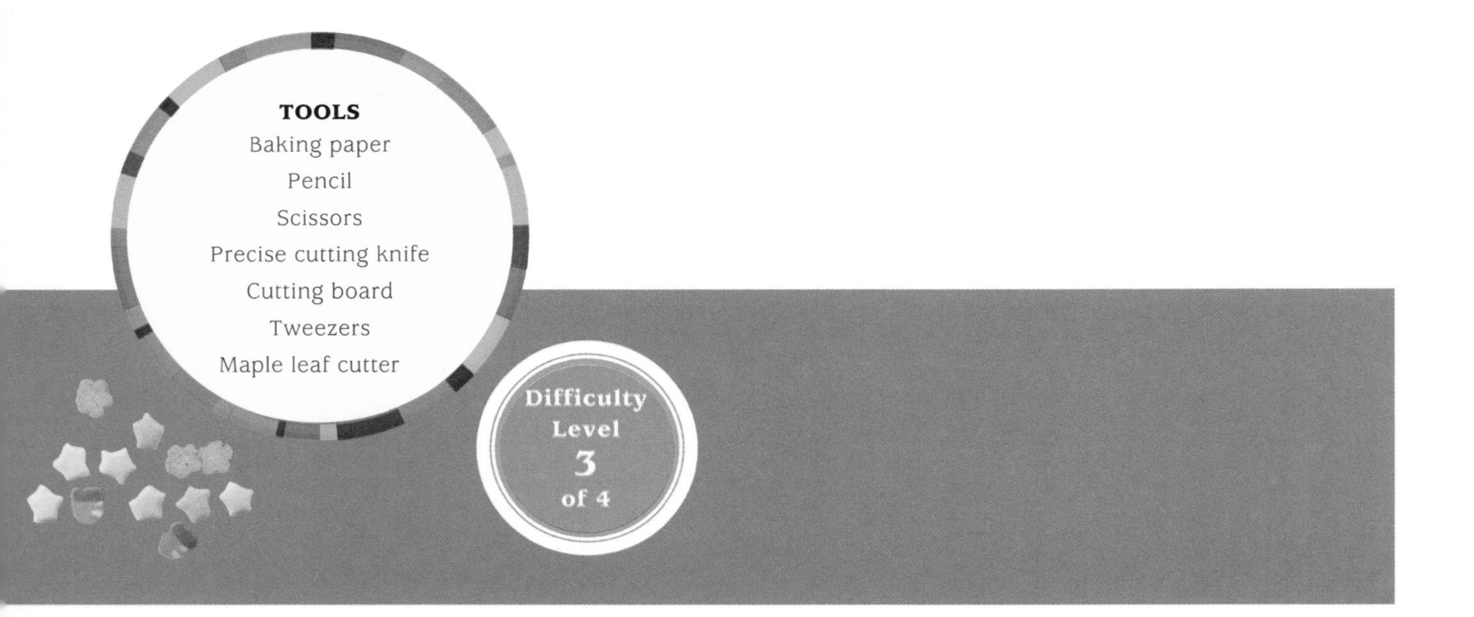

Winter Wonderland 冬のキャラ弁

Character Bento

150–180 g cooked Japanese short-grain rice (page 20)

1 slice carrot, boiled

1 seaweed sheet

1 crabstick (*kani kamaboko*)

1/2 slice Japanese fish cake (*hanpen*)

Side Dishes

Fried chicken drumsticks

Vegetables of choice

Fresh fruit

1. Take 1 Tbsp cooked rice and shape it into 2 flat circles using cling wrap. Have one slightly larger than the other for the snowman's body. Set aside.
2. Using a small straw, cut out 2 circles for the snowman's buttons from the carrot. Using a knife, cut a small thin triangle for the snowman's nose from the remaining carrot. Set aside.
3. Using a pair of scissors, cut the seaweed to fit the bento box. Cut circles for the eyes and a curved line for the mouth from the remaining seaweed. Set aside.
4. Spoon three-quarters of the remaining cooked rice into the bento box.
5. Place the seaweed sheet on the rice. Arrange the reserved rice loosely around the sides.
6. Assemble the snowman on the seaweed.
7. Cut a red strip for the scarf from the crabstick and place it on the snowman. Using a pair of tweezers, place the eyes, mouth, nose and buttons on the snowman. Stick a bento pick into the snowman for the hat.
8. Using a snowflake cutter, cut out snowflakes from the fish cake and place on the bento.
9. Complete the bento meal with side dishes such as fried chicken drumsticks, vegetables of choice and fresh fruit.

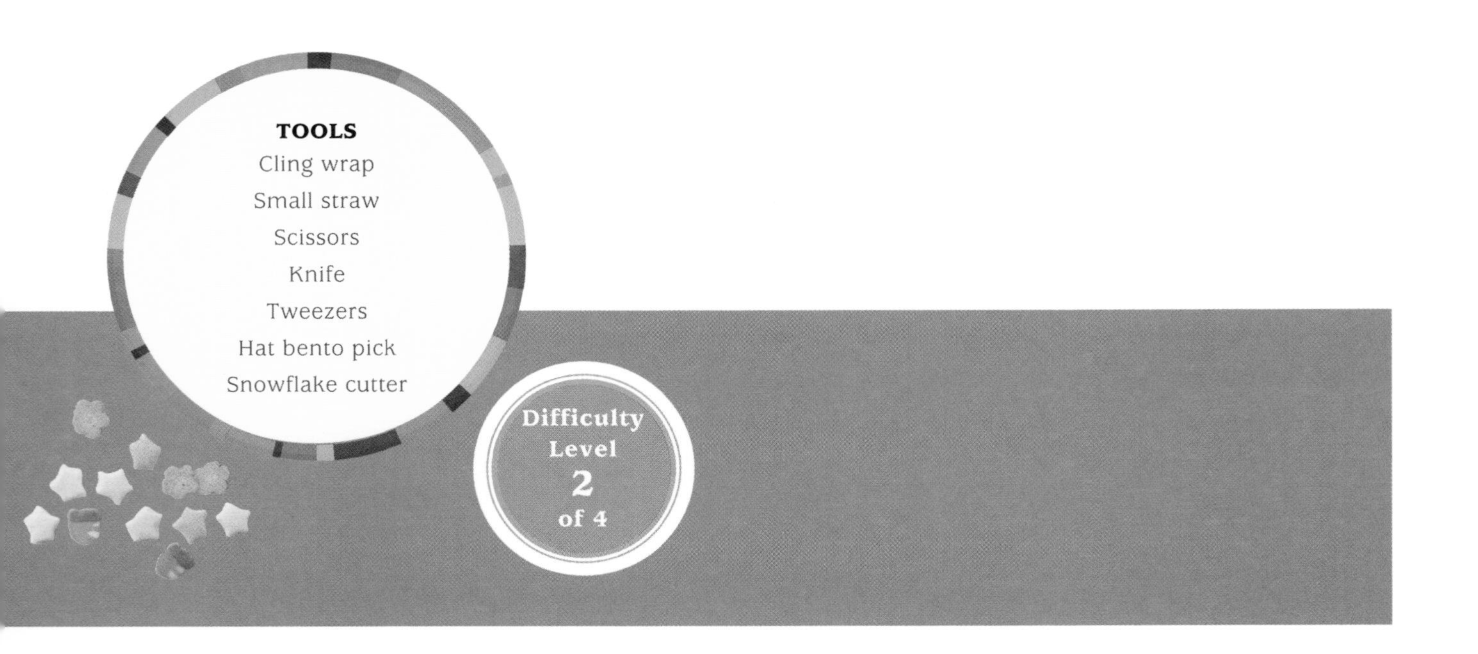

ABC
IT'S A GIRL!
IT'S A BOY!

Special Occasion Bentos

Baby Shower 56

Birthday Gift Box 58

Marital Bliss 60

Graduation Day 62

Baby Shower おねんね赤ちゃんのキャラ弁

Character Bento

120–130 g cooked Japanese short-grain rice (page 20)

1/2 tsp teriyaki sauce

1/4 seaweed sheet

1/4 yellow egg sheet (page 26)

1/4 orange egg sheet (page 26)

2 pasta sticks, each about 2 cm

1/2 tsp bonito flakes (*katsuobushi*)

2 ribbon pasta, boiled

Side Dishes

Lettuce

Stir-fried prawns

Vegetables of choice

Fresh fruit

1. Mix the rice evenly with teriyaki sauce to add colour to the faces. Divide the rice into 2 equal parts. Using cling wrap, shape two-thirds of each portion into a round for the heads. Shape the remaining portions into ovals for the bodies.
2. Using a seaweed punch, cut out the eyes and noses from seaweed. Set aside.
3. Using a star cutter, cut out some stars from the yellow and orange egg sheets. Set aside.
4. Decorate the blankets with the star cut-outs.
5. Line the bento box with lettuce. Position the larger rice balls in the bento box for the heads and the oval rice balls for the bodies.
6. Using tweezers, place the seaweed eyes and mouths on the faces.
7. Sprinkle some bonito flakes on the heads for hair.
8. Wrap the yellow egg sheet around an oval rice ball for the baby's blanket and secure with a pasta stick. Place it into the bento box. Do the same with the orange egg sheet.
9. Decorate the bento with bento picks and boiled ribbon pasta.
10. Complete the bento meal with side dishes such as stir-fried prawns, vegetables of choice and fresh fruit.

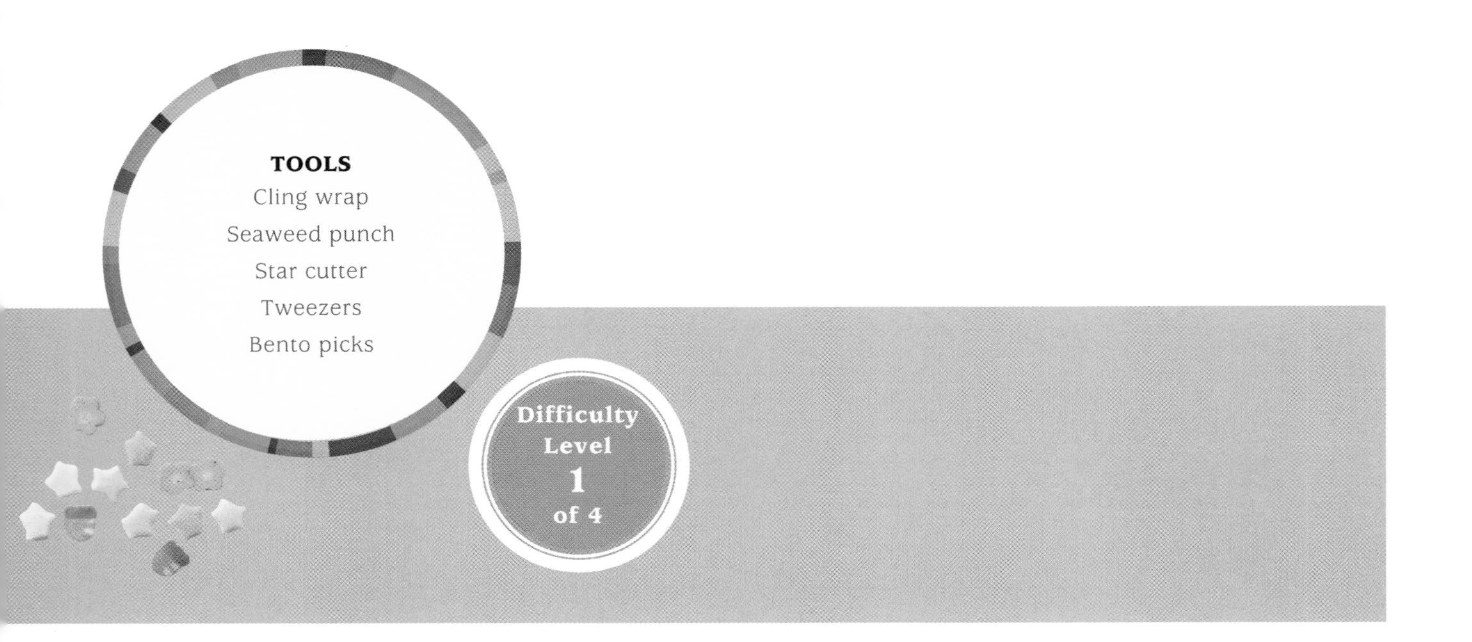

IT'S A GIRL!
IT'S A BOY!

Birthday Gift Box お誕生日のキャラ弁

Character Bento

2 slices sandwich bread

2 Tbsp sandwich filling of choice

1/4 brown egg sheet (page 26)

1/4 yellow egg sheet (page 26)

1/4 orange egg sheet (page 26)

1/4 green egg sheet (page 26)

1 slice ham

1 pasta stick, about 2 cm, deep-fried

Side Dishes

Tamago cakes (page 107)

Fresh fruit

1. Spread the bread with a filling of choice to make a sandwich. Place the sandwich in the bento box.
2. Using a round cutter, cut out circles from the brown egg sheet. Using a smaller round cutter, cut out circles from the coloured egg sheets. Set aside.
3. Cut 4 strips for the ribbon from the ham. Halve one of the strips and cut a notch on one end for the tail of the ribbon.
4. Cut a wide figure of 8 out of the remaining ham. Pinch the centre of the ham to form a bow. Wrap a strip of ham around the bow and secure with the pasta stick. Trim off the excess ham.
5. Arrange the ham ribbon on the sandwich to create the look of a gift box.
6. Place the brown egg sheet circles on the sandwiches to form a polka dot pattern. Place the coloured egg sheet circles on the brown circles.
7. Complete the bento meal with *tamago* cakes and fresh fruit.

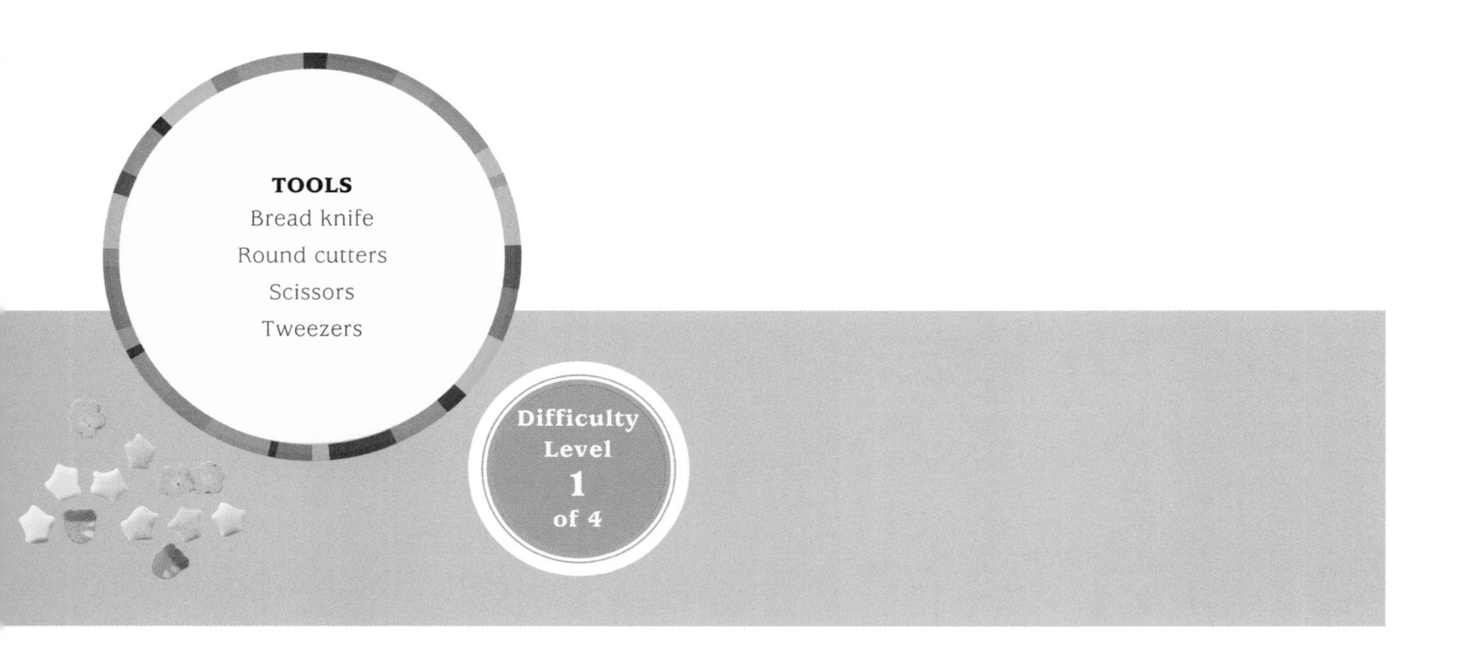

Marital Bliss 仲良し夫婦のキャラ弁

Character Bento

2 slices chicken ham

1 egg white sheet (page 26)

1 brown egg sheet (page 26)

1 seaweed sheet

150–180 g cooked Japanese short-grain rice (page 20)

A little mayonnaise

5 pieces flower character rice topping (character *furikake*)

4 white multicolour rice crackers (*arare*)

A little crabstick (*kani kamaboko*), red layer

Side Dishes

Pan-fried salmon fillet

Vegetables of choice

Fresh fruit

1. Trace the drawing of the bride and groom (page 118) on a sheet of baking paper. Trace the parts (body, head, clothes and hair) separately as you will need to cut the different layers (page 29).
2. Using a pair of scissors, cut out the sections.
3. Place the body cut-outs on the chicken ham and cut using a precise cutting knife.
4. Place the head cut-outs on the remaining chicken ham and cut using a precise cutting knife.
5. Place the dress cut-out on the egg white sheet and cut using a precise cutting knife.
6. Place the hair cut-outs on the brown egg sheet and cut using a precise cutting knife.
7. Place the groom's outfit cut-outs on the remaining chicken ham and cut using a precise cutting knife. Place a sheet of seaweed over the ham and trim off the excess to create the dark suit.
8. Using a seaweed punch or a pair of scissors, cut 6 curved lines for the eyes and mouths from the remaining seaweed.
9. Spoon the cooked rice into the bento box. Using a pair of tweezers, assemble the pieces and layers on the rice. Dab a little mayonnaise on the ingredients to secure the layers.
10. Using a clover cutter, cut out a clover for the bride's bouquet from the green egg sheet. Place on the bride, then decorate with flowers from the flower character rice topping. Place some of the flowers on the bride's hair.
11. Using a pair of tweezers, give the bride a string of pearls with the white multicolour rice crackers.
12. Using a pair of scissors, cut 2 small triangles for the groom's brooch from the crabstick and place on the groom's suit.
13. Complete the bento meal with side dishes such as pan-fried salmon fillet, vegetables of choice and fresh fruit.

TOOLS

Baking paper
Pencil
Scissors
Precise cutting knife
Cutting board
Seaweed punch
Tweezers
Clover cutter

Difficulty Level 3 of 4

Graduation Day 卒業式のキャラ弁

Character Bento

2 Tbsp Japanese light soy sauce

1 Tbsp mirin

1/2 tsp sugar

1 medium egg

1 egg white sheet

3 pasta sticks, each about 2 cm

1 1/2 seaweed sheets

1 slice mini sausage, about 1-cm thick

A little ham

1 slice carrot

150–180 g cooked Japanese short-grain rice (page 20)

Egg sheet graduation scroll (page 107)

Side Dishes

Roast chicken

Japanese egg roll (*tamagoyaki*)

Vegetables of choice

1. Combine the soy sauce, mirin and sugar in a jar or small deep bowl. Mix to dissolve the sugar. Set aside.
2. Place the egg in a saucepan filled with water. Bring to the boil and cook for 7–8 minutes.
3. Remove the hard-boiled egg and peel. Place the egg in the soy sauce mixture and let soak until the desired colour is achieved. As only about three-quarters of the egg will be submerged, part of the egg will be lighter in colour. Use this part for the owl's breast.
4. Cut the egg in half, keeping the owl's breast intact. From the other portion of the egg, cut out 2 small pieces for the owl's wings and 2 small triangles for the ears tufts.
5. Using a round cutter, cut out 2 circles for the owl's eyes from the egg white sheet.
6. To make the graduation hat, wrap a small sheet of seaweed around the slice of sausage. Cut the ham into a small triangle and wrap with seaweed. Attach this flat piece to the round piece using the pasta stick. Secure the hat to the owl using the pasta stick as well.
7. Using a knife, cut the carrot into a triangle for the owl's beak.
8. Using a seaweed punch or a pair of scissors, cut 6 curved lines for feathers on the owl's breast, and 2 larger curved lines for the eyes from seaweed.
9. Using a pair of tweezers, assemble the owl's eyes, feathers and beak. Attach the ear tufts and wings using the pasta stick.
10. Spoon the cooked rice into the bento box. Place the owl on the rice. Decorate the bento with an egg sheet graduation scroll and blackboard bento pick.
11. Complete the bento meal with side dishes such as roast chicken, egg roll and vegetables of choice.

TOOLS

Knife

Round cutter

Scissors

Tweezers

Seaweed punch

Blackboard bento pick

Difficulty Level 2 of 4

ABC

Festival & Celebration Bentos

Mother's Day 66

Father's Day 68

National Day 70

Halloween 72

Christmas 74

Mother's Day 母の日のキャラ弁

Character Bento

1 small beetroot

400 ml water

4 pieces farfelle pasta

2 thin asparagus spears, boiled

1 green pea, boiled

2 pasta sticks, each about 2 cm

150–180 g cooked Japanese short-grain rice (page 20)

1 yellow udon noodle stick, boiled

Side Dishes

Meat croquette

Vegetables of choice

Fresh fruit

1. The farfelle pasta is coloured pink using beetroot. To do this, peel and cut the beetroot into small cubes. Place in a saucepan with the water and bring to the boil. Let boil for a few seconds, then turn off the heat. Strain the liquid and discard the beet.
2. Add the farfelle pasta to the pan and boil for about 7 minutes until the pasta is a lovely shade of pink. Remove from the pan.
3. Cut the pasta pieces in half. Make the flowers by placing one half on another half and using 4 halves for each flower.
4. Cut the asparagus to the length required for the flower stalks.
5. Cut 2 short sections from the green pea at a diagonal. Open the pod so it resembles the sepal of a flower. Place over the cut ends of the pasta and secure with a pasta stick.
6. Spoon the cooked rice into the bento box. Arrange the flowers on the rice. Make a ribbon with the yellow udon noodle and place on the flowers.
7. Complete the bento meal with side dishes such as meat croquettes, vegetables of choice and fresh fruit.

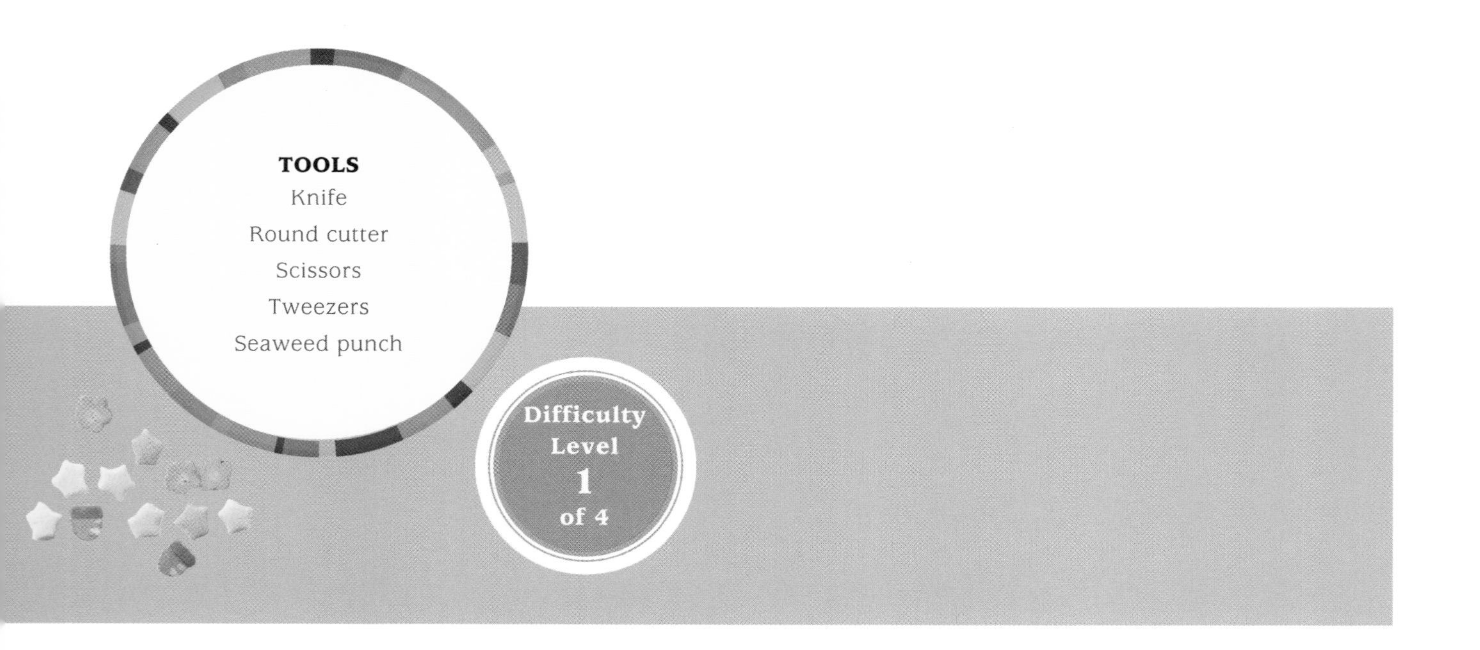

Father's Day 父の日のキャラ弁

Character Bento

170–190 g cooked Japanese short-grain rice (page 20)

1 packet blue deco rice topping (deco *furikake*)

½ tsp teriyaki sauce

1½ seaweed sheets

¼ egg white sheet (page 26)

¼ orange egg sheet (page 26)

1 red egg sheet (page 26)

A little ham

2 heart-shaped pasta, boiled

Side Dishes

Stir-fried meat

Vegetables of choice

1. Place 1½ Tbsp cooked rice in a bowl and mix with blue deco rice topping.
2. Add teriyaki sauce to the remaining rice and mix well. Using cling wrap, shape 1 Tbsp rice for the girl's body and 1 tsp rice for the girl's arm.
3. Shape the remaining rice into 2 rounds, a larger round for the father's head and a smaller one for the girl's head. Set aside.
4. Using a pair of scissors, cut out a wide inverted V for the father's fringe from one end of the larger sheet of seaweed, then cut the other side into a curve. Place it on the large rice ball and cut slits around the curved side of the seaweed, so it sits nicely around the rice ball for the father's hair (page 22). Cover with cling wrap. Set aside.
5. From the smaller sheet of seaweed, cut a semicircle. On the straight side, cut out a square for the girl's fringe. Make slits around the curved side, so it sits nicely around the rice ball (page 22). Cover with cling wrap and set aside.
6. Using a pair of scissors, cut 2 circles for the girl's eyes, 4 curved lines for the father's eyes and both the mouths, and a smaller curve for the father's nose from the remaining seaweed.
7. Using cling wrap, shape the blue rice from step 1 into the shirt for the father.
8. Trim and cut the egg white sheet and orange egg sheet for the father's collar and necktie.
9. Cut a strip of red egg sheet and wrap it around the rice ball for the girl's arm. Use the remaining red egg sheet and wrap it around the girl's body.
10. Using a small straw, cut out 2 circles for the girl's cheeks from ham.
11. Assemble the girl and father in the bento box. Using a pair of tweezers, place the features on the characters. Place a panda bear bento pick in the girl's arm.
12. Complete the bento meal with side dishes such as stir-fried meat and vegetables of choice. Finish with the heart-shaped pasta and more fun bento picks.

TOOLS

Cling wrap

Scissors

Knife

Straw

Tweezers

Panda bear bento pick

Difficulty Level 3 of 4

National Day ナショナルデーのキャラ弁

Character Bento

160–180 g cooked Japanese short-grain rice (page 20)

2 crabsticks (*kani kamaboko*)

1 egg white sheet (page 26)

Side Dishes

Boiled chicken

Grilled spicy fish cake (*otak-otak*)

Vegetables of choice

1. Using cling wrap, shape and mould the rice into a rectangular shape to fit the bento box.
2. Using a knife, make a slit along the side of each crabstick. Peel open and tear away the white layer, leaving the red layer. Trim away any white areas.
3. Place the red crabstick layers on the rice, overlapping the layers, so the red part of the flag is completely red.
4. Using a precise cutting knife, trace and cut out a crescent moon from the egg white sheet.
5. Using a star cutter, cut out 5 stars from the egg white sheet.
6. Using a pair of tweezers, place the crescent moon and stars on the red part of the flag.
7. Complete the bento meal with side dishes such as boiled chicken and vegetables of choice. Finish with a home-made Singapore flag bento pick.

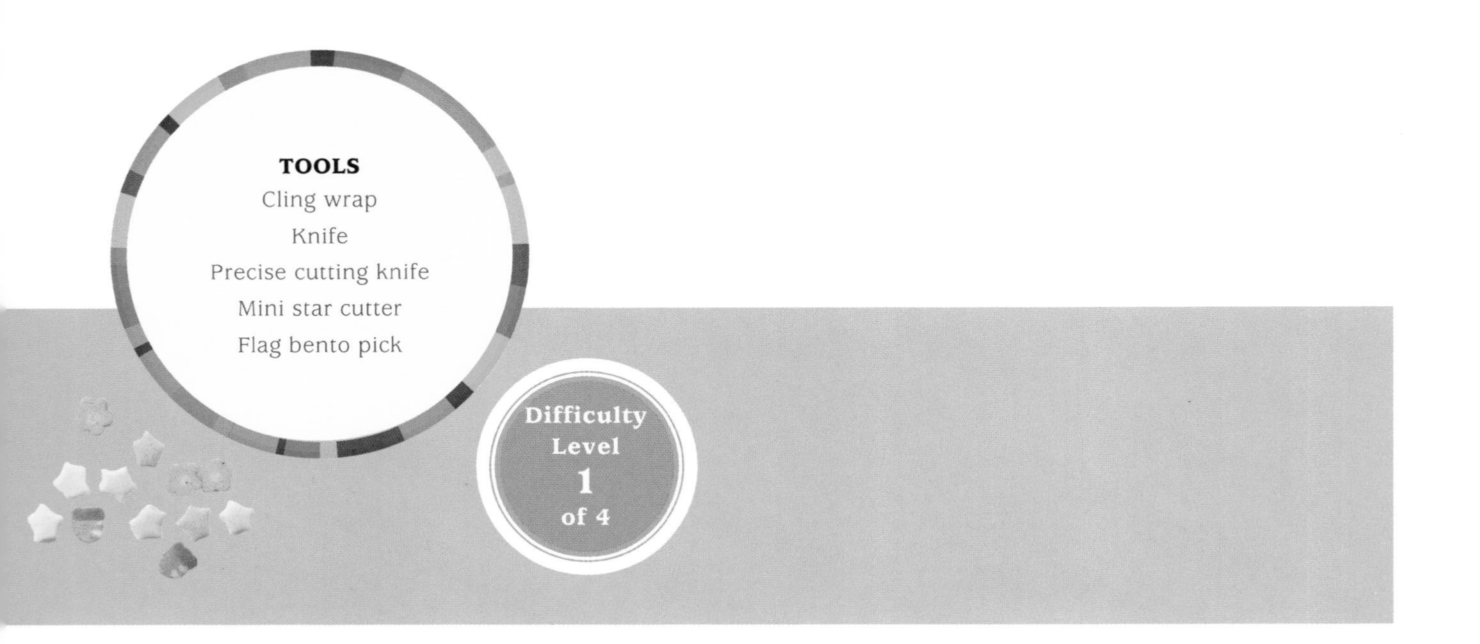

Halloween ハロウィンのキャラ弁

Character Bento

1/2 cup edamame beans, boiled

70–80 g cooked Japanese short-grain rice (page 20)

1 seaweed sheet

1/4 egg white sheet (page 26)

1/2 cup pumpkin, boiled and mashed

Salt to taste

1/2 slice ham

A thin slice of cucumber, skin intact

1 quail egg ghost (page 111)

1 seaweed bat (page 109)

Side Dishes

Pan-fried meat patties

Vegetables of choice

TOOLS

Food processor

Cling wrap

Spatula/spoon

Scissors

Seaweed punch

Scraper

Tweezers

Star cutter

1. Remove the edamame beans from the pods and squeeze the beans from the skin. Place in a food processor and process into a paste. Set aside.
2. Using cling wrap, shape the cooked rice into an rectangular shape with rounded edges for Frankenstein's head.
3. Using a small spatula or the back of a spoon, spread the edamame bean paste over the rice, covering the front and sides of the rice ball. Cover with cling wrap and rub the surface gently to smoothen the bean paste layer. Remove the cling wrap.
4. Using a pair of scissors, cut a semicircle from the seaweed sheet. Make the straight edge jagged for Frankenstein's hair. Place it on Frankenstein's head and cut slits around the curved side of the seaweed, so it sits nicely around the head (page 22). Cover with cling wrap and set aside.
5. From the remaining seaweed, cut lines for the scar and eyebrows, and a curved line for the mouth.
6. Using a seaweed punch, cut 2 circles for Frankenstein's eyes from seaweed. Using a pair of scissors, cut small squares for the white of Frankenstein's eyes from the egg white sheet.
7. Season the mashed pumpkin with a little salt if desired. Using cling wrap, shape the pumpkin mash into an oval, then use a scraper or a tool with thin flat ends to make indentations to create a jack-o'-lantern.
8. Using a pair of scissors, cut triangles for the eyes and a jagged shape for the mouth of the jack-o'-lantern from the remaining seaweed.
9. Assemble Frankenstein and the jack-o'-lantern in the bento box. Using a pair of tweezers, place the features on Frankenstein and the jack-o'-lantern.
10. Cut a rectangular piece for the stem of the jack-o'-lantern from the Japanese cucumber. Place it on the top of the jack-o'-lantern.
11. Complete the bento meal with side dishes such as pan-fried meat patties and vegetables of choice. Using a star cutter, cut stars out of ham and decorate the bento. Finish with a quail egg ghost and seaweed bat.

Difficulty Level 1 of 4

Christmas クリスマスのキャラ弁

Character Bento

1 quail egg

1 slice cheese

1/2 egg white sheet (page 26)

1/2 seaweed sheet

A little yellow egg sheet (page 26)

A little mayonnaise

1 white multicolour rice cracker (*arare*)

2 dinner rolls

Lettuce

2 Tbsp sandwich filling

4 slices carrot, boiled

1 mini red sausage

2 pasta sticks, each about 2 cm

Side Dishes

3 *tamago* gift boxes (page 107)

2 ham flowers (page 106)

Fresh fruit

TOOLS

Knife

Scissors

Round cutter

Straw

Seaweed punch

Precise cutting knife

Tweezers

Difficulty Level 2 of 4

1. Hard-boil and colour the quail egg dark pink (page 25).
2. Using a knife, cut a thin slice off the narrow end of the quail egg, then cut a small triangle from it for Santa's hat.
3. Using a round cutter, cut a circle for Santa's face from cheese. Using a small straw, cut a small circle for Santa's nose from the cheese as well.
4. Using a pair of scissors, cut a triangle for Santa's beard and two thin strips for his eyebrows from the white egg sheet.
5. Using a seaweed punch, cut curved lines for Santa's eyes from the seaweed. Using a pair of scissors, cut a thin strip of seaweed for Santa's belt.
6. Using a precise cutting knife, cut a small square for Santa's buckle from the yellow egg sheet.
7. Using a pair of tweezers assemble Santa. Dab a little mayonnaise on the ingredients to secure the layers. Finish his hat with a white multicolour rice cracker. Set aside.
8. Make a slit in the top of the dinner rolls and fill with lettuce and sandwich filling. Arrange in the bento box.
9. Using a knife, cut antlers for the reindeer from the carrot slices.
10. Using a round cutter, cut 4 circles for the white of the reindeers' eyes from cheese. Using a pair of scissors or a seaweed punch, cut 2 circles and 2 curved lines for the eyes from seaweed.
11. Using a knife, cut off the ends of the mini sausage for the reindeers' noses.
12. Using a pair of tweezers, place the reindeer's eyes on the dinner rolls. Stick the antlers into the rolls. Position the noses using pasta sticks.
13. Complete the bento meal with side dishes such as *tamago* gift boxes, ham flowers and fresh fruit.

Merry
CHRISTMAS

Animal & Nature Themed Bentos

Panda in a Bamboo Forest 78

Woolly Rams 80

Baby Chicks 82

Sunshine Bear 84

Sleeping Bunnies 86

Happy Cow 88

Best Friends 90

Lady Bug 92

Panda in a Bamboo Forest パンダさんのキャラ弁

Character Bento

120 g cooked Japanese short-grain rice (page 20)

1 seaweed sheet

A little pink Japanese fish roll (*kamaboko*)

2 pasta sticks, each about 2 cm

Green bean bamboo (page 110)

Side Dishes

Lettuce

Sweet potato flowers (page 106)

Pan-fried meatballs

1. Using cling wrap, shape about three-quarters of the cooked rice into a ball. You can add some filling to the rice ball at this point, if desired (page 21). This will be the panda's head.
2. Shape two-thirds of the remaining rice into an oval for the panda's body. Divide the rest into 4 portions and shape 2 portions into balls for the ears and the other 2 into ovals for the limbs.
3. Using a pair of scissors, cut 2 circles large enough to wrap around the ears from the seaweed. Cut slits around the sides and wrap the seaweed around the balls. Cover with cling wrap and set aside.
4. Similarly, cut 2 ovals large enough to wrap around the limbs from the seaweed. Cut slits around the sides and wrap the seaweed around the limbs. Cover with cling wrap and set aside.
5. Cut 2 ovals for the eyes and a V-shape for the mouth from the remaining seaweed.
6. Using a straw, cut 2 circles for the panda's cheeks from the pink portion of the Japanese fish roll.
7. Assemble the panda in the bento box. Attach the ears using pasta sticks if necessary. Using a pair of tweezers, place the eyes, mouth and cheeks on the panda.
8. Complete the bento meal with a green bean bamboo forest and side dishes such as lettuce, sweet potato flowers and pan-fried meatballs skewered with bamboo picks and decorated with string or ribbon.

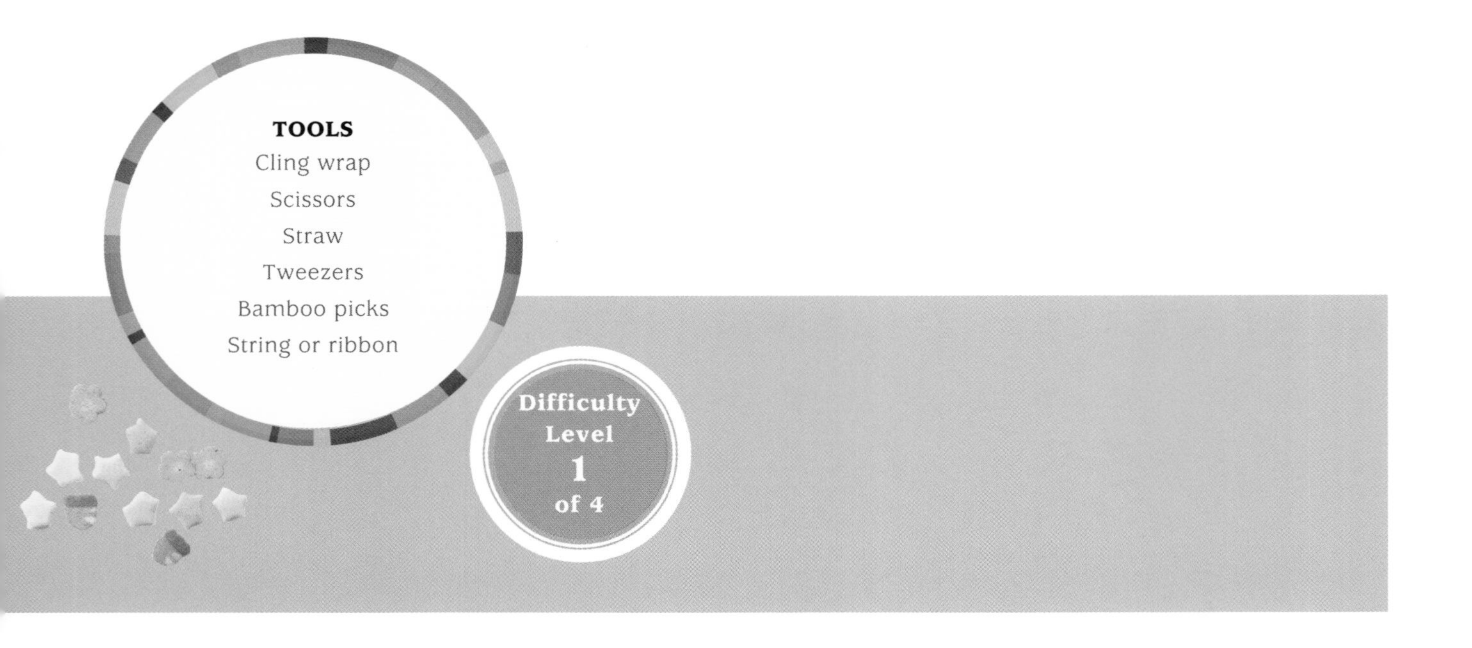

Woolly Rams 羊さんのキャラ弁

Character Bento

180 g cooked Japanese short-grain rice (page 20)

1 tsp teriyaki sauce

¼ seaweed sheet

A little pink Japanese fish roll (*kamaboko*)

¼ brown egg sheet (page 26)

Side Dishes

Deep-fried breaded prawns

Vegetables of choice

Fresh fruit

1. Mix about one-fifth of the rice evenly with teriyaki sauce. Divide the rice into 3 portions. Using cling wrap, shape 2 portions into ovals for the heads of the rams. Divide the remaining portion into 4 and shape into oblongs for the legs.
2. Assemble the heads in the bento box and spoon the unflavoured rice loosely into the box to form the bodies. Position the legs using chopsticks.
3. Using a pair of scissors, cut 2 circles and 2 curved lines for the eyes, 2 small circles for the noses, and 2 small lines and 2 curved lines for the mouths from seaweed.
4. Using a straw, cut 2 circles for the rams' cheeks from the pink portion of the Japanese fish roll.
5. Using a round cutter, cut 2 circles from the brown egg sheet. Using a pair of scissors, trim the circles to form the rams' horns.
6. Using a pair of tweezers, place the eyes, noses, mouths, cheeks and horns on the rams.
7. Complete the bento meal with side dishes such as deep-fried breaded prawns, vegetables of choice and fresh fruit. Decorate with bento picks if desired.

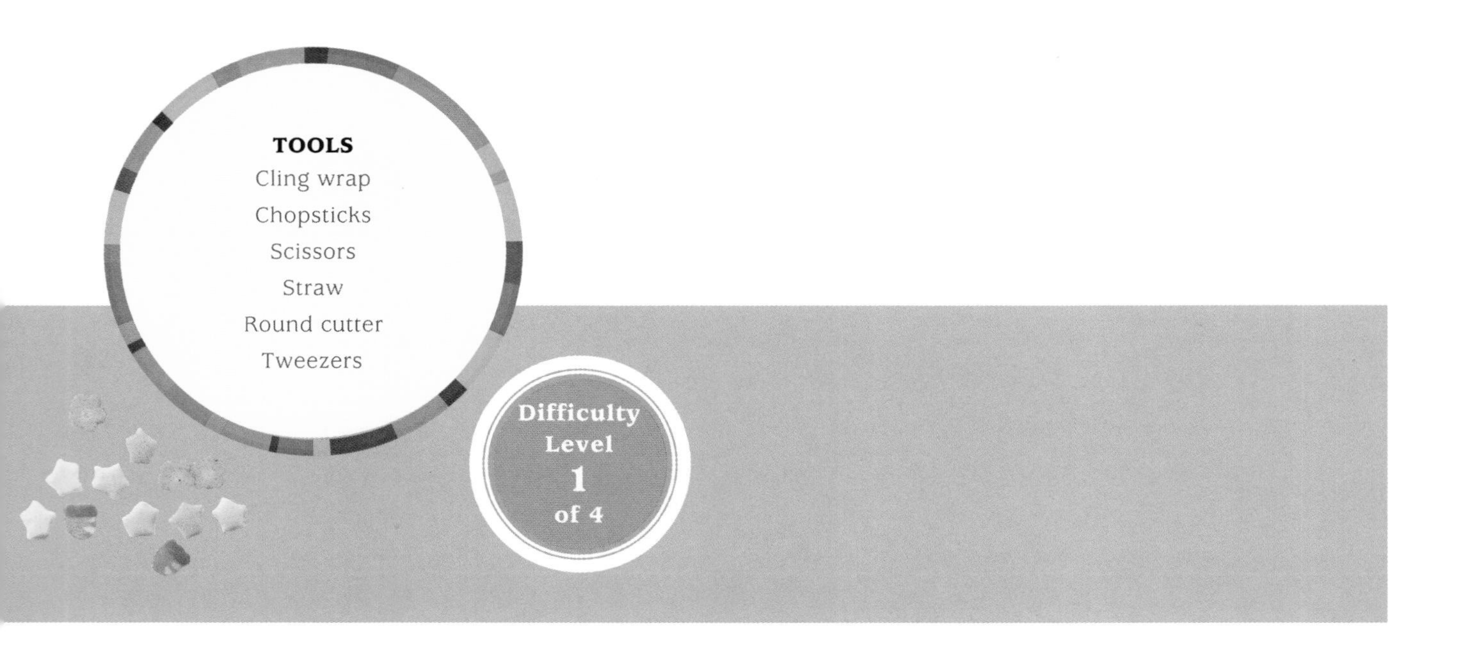

Baby Chicks にわとりさんのキャラ弁

Character Bento

160 g cooked Japanese short-grain rice (page 20)

Japanese egg *soboro* (page 42) or 1 hard-boiled egg yolk from a large egg

1 slice carrot, boiled

1/4 seaweed sheet

Lettuce

Side Dishes

Baked chicken drumlets

Grilled prawns

Vegetables of choice

Edamame beans

1. Mix the rice evenly with the egg *soboro* or hard-boiled egg yolk.
2. Using cling wrap, shape the rice into 2 balls. Set aside.
3. Using an oval cutter, cut 2 ovals for the beaks from the carrot.
4. Using a pair of scissors, cut 4 circles for the eyes and 4 rounded Ws for the feet from seaweed.
5. Using tweezers, place the eyes and feet on the chicks. Finish by inserting red heart bento picks for the comb.
6. Place some lettuce in the bento box and assemble the chicks.
7. Complete the bento meal with side dishes such as baked chicken drumlets, grilled prawns and vegetables of choice.
8. Decorate with edamame beans skewered with chick bento picks.

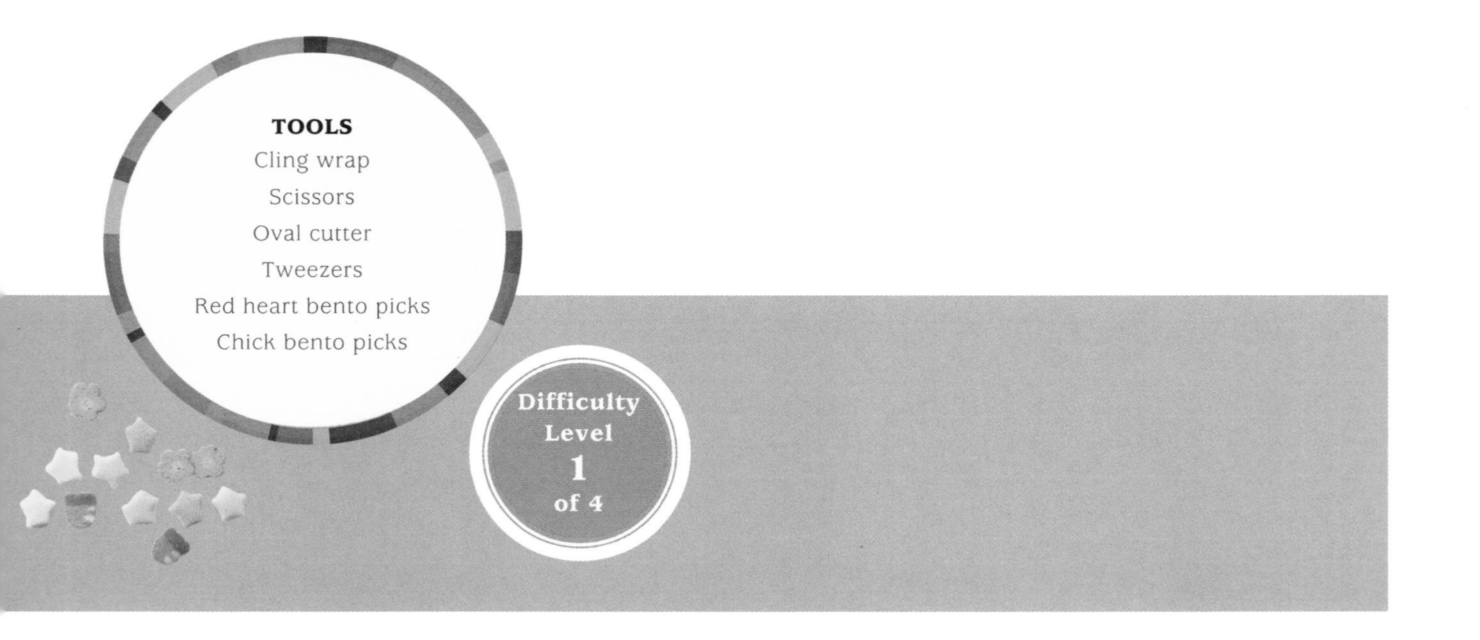

TOOLS

Cling wrap

Scissors

Oval cutter

Tweezers

Red heart bento picks

Chick bento picks

Sunshine Bear 熊さんのキャラ弁

Character Bento

Cooking oil, as needed

2 Japanese fried round fish cakes (*satsuma-age*)

A little cheddar cheese

1/4 seaweed sheet

160 g cooked Japanese short-grain rice (page 20)

2 pasta sticks, each about 2 cm

1 edamame bean

Side Dishes

Sausage egg sunflower (page 108)

Stir-fried prawns

Vegetables of choice

1. Lightly oil a frying pan over medium heat. Add the fish cakes and cook until golden brown on both sides.
2. Using a round cutter, cut out 2 circles for the bear's ears from one of the fish cakes. Using a knife, trim the circles to shape them into ears.
3. Using a smaller round cutter, cut a circle from the cheddar cheese, then halve it for the inner ears.
4. Using a pair of scissors, cut 2 circles for the eyes and a curved line for the mouth from seaweed.
5. Spoon the cooked rice into the bento box and place the whole fish cake in the box.
6. Insert the ears using pasta sticks. Using tweezers, place the inner ears, eyes and mouth on the bear. Place the edamame bean for the nose.
7. Complete the bento meal with side dishes such as sausage egg sunflower, stir-fried prawns and vegetables of choice.
8. Decorate with edamame beans skewered with leaf bento picks.

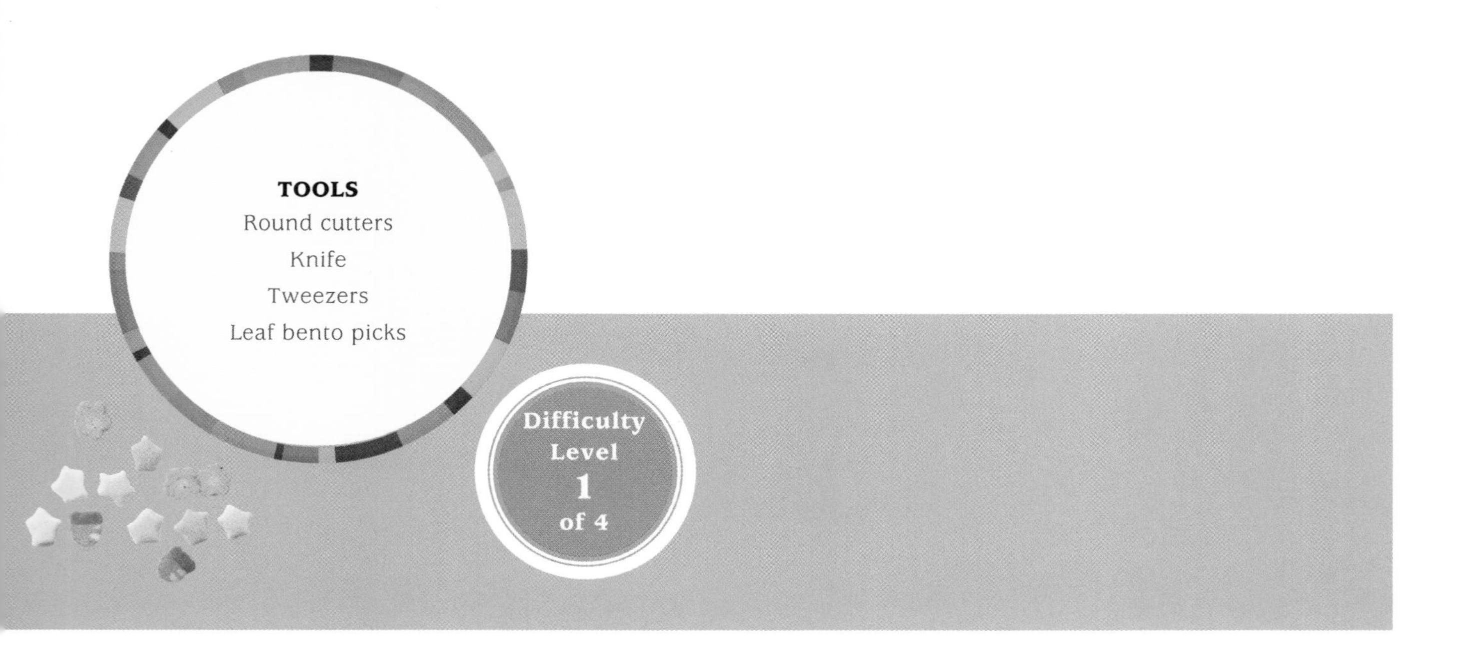

Sleeping Bunnies 夢見るうさぎさんのキャラ弁

Character Bento

2 large eggs

1/2 tsp potato starch, mixed with 1 tsp water

Cooking oil, as needed

4 quail eggs

6 pasta sticks, each about 2 cm

3-cm slice pink Japanese fish roll (*kamaboko*)

1/4 seaweed sheet

Lettuce

2 slices plain sandwich bread, toasted

Side Dishes

2 tomato roses (page 111)

Fried chicken cubes

TOOLS

Sieve

Star Cutter

Cutting board

Knife

Seaweed punch

Tweezers

Bunny bento picks

Difficulty Level 2 of 4

1. Separate the white and yolk of a large egg. To the egg yolk, add another egg and beat.
2. To the egg white, add the potato starch mixture and mix well. Strain with a fine sieve and set aside.
3. Lightly oil a frying pan and place over low heat. Pour the egg yolk mixture from Step 1 into the pan. Cover and cook until the sides of the egg sheet are done. Turn off the heat and let sit for 20–30 seconds for the egg sheet to finish cooking in the residual heat. Remove the egg sheet from the pan.
4. Using a star cutter, make random cut-outs on the egg sheet. Reserve the cut-outs for decorating the bento.
5. Return the egg sheet to the pan. Carefully pour the egg white mixture from Step 2 into the star shape cut-outs. Turn on low heat and cover the pan until the egg white is cooked.
6. Place the quail eggs in a saucepan filled with water. Bring to the boil and cook for 6–7 minutes.
7. Remove the hard-boiled quail eggs and peel.
8. Choose 2 of the rounder quail eggs and gently mould them for the bunnies' heads. This is best done while the eggs are still warm. Use the rounder side for the face.
9. Attach each head to another quail egg for the bodies.
10. Line the bento box with lettuce, then add the toasted bread. Assemble the quail eggs and egg sheet on the toast.
11. Using a knife, cut 4 ears and 4 paws for the bunnies from the white portion of the Japanese fish roll. Attach the ears to the heads using pasta sticks. Cut 4 inner ears from pink portion of the Japanese fish roll. Arrange the inner ears and paws.
12. Using a seaweed punch, cut 4 eyes, 2 noses, a mouth and a line for the bunnies from seaweed.
13. Using a pair of tweezers, place the features on the bunnies. Dab a little mayonnaise on the parts to secure them to the egg.
14. Complete the bento meal with the star cut-outs, and side dishes such as tomato roses and fried chicken cubes.
15. Add a bunny bento pick to enhance the look of the bento.

Happy Cow 牛さんのキャラ弁

Character Bento

100–120 g cooked Japanese short-grain rice (page 20)

1 seaweed sheet

A little pink Japanese fish roll (*kamaboko*)

Lettuce

Alfalfa sprouts

Side Dishes

3 deco sausages (page 109)

Fried meat roll

Vegetables of choice

Fresh fruit

1. Divide the cooked rice into 2 portions.
2. Divide one of the portions into 2 parts. Using cling wrap, shape one part into a flat oval for the cow's muzzle. Take 1 tsp from the other part and shape into 2 triangular ears. Shape the other part of the rice into an oval for the cow's head.
3. Using cling wrap, shape the second portion of rice to form the body and legs of the cow.
4. Using a pair of scissors, cut 2 ovals for the eyes, 2 circles for the patches on the cow, and a curved line for the mouth from seaweed.
5. Using a seaweed punch, cut 2 small circles for the cow's nostrils from seaweed.
6. Using a round cutter or straw, cut 2 circles for the cow's cheeks from the pink layer of the Japanese fish roll.
7. Using a knife, cut 2 small triangles for the cow's inner ears from the pink layer of the Japanese fish roll, and a tail from the white layer of the Japanese fish roll.
8. Fill the bento box with lettuce and alfalfa sprouts and assemble the cow. Using a pair of tweezers, place the features on the cow.
9. Complete the bento meal with side dishes such as deco sausages, fried meat roll, vegetables of choice and fresh fruit.

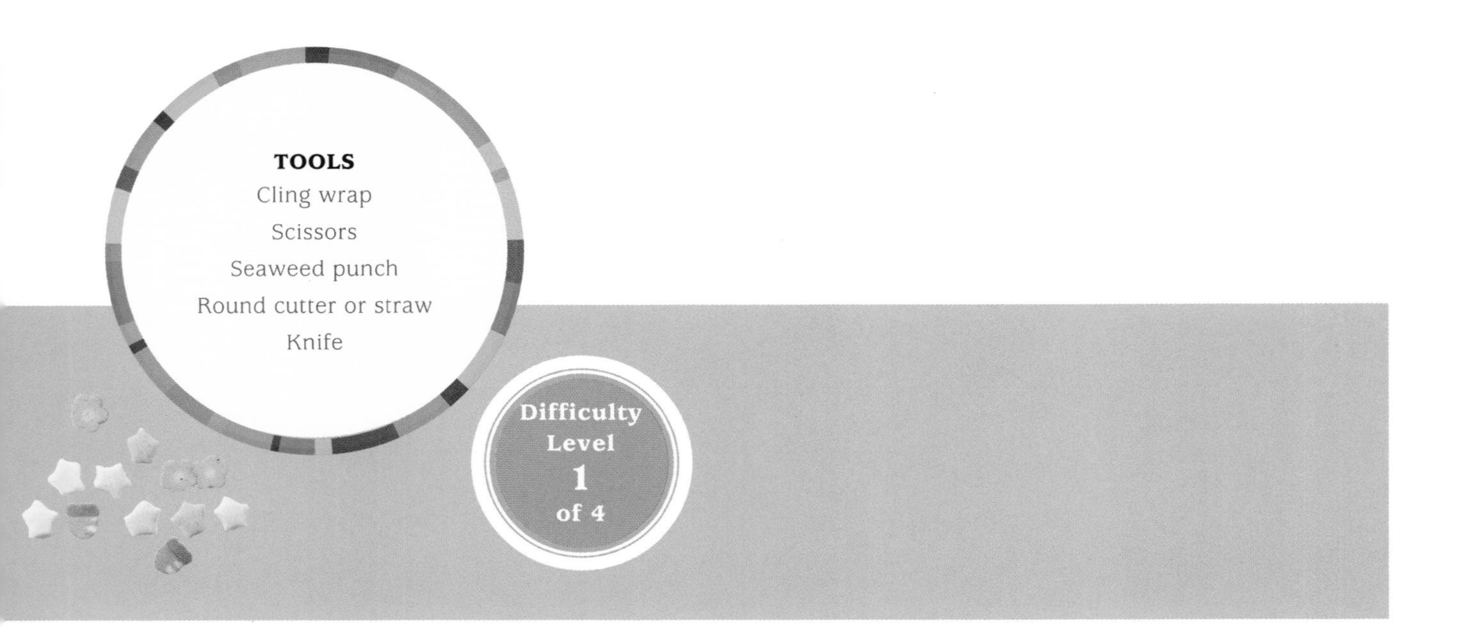

Best Friends 虎さんのキャラ弁

Character Bento

3 hamburger buns

1/2 seaweed sheet

2 Tbsp sandwich filling

Lettuce

1 tomato, sliced

1/2 Japanese cucumber, sliced

A little mayonnaise

A little ketchup

Side Dishes

2 checked apples (page 110)

Fried breaded prawns

1. Using a knife, slice the buns into halves.
2. Using a pair of scissors, cut 2 triangles for the tiger's ears, 2 circles for the koala's ears and an oval for the koala's nose from one of the top halves of the buns.
3. Flatten the remaining part of the bun and cut 2 small triangles for the tiger's inner ears and 2 small tulip-shaped pieces for the koala's inner ears from the white side of the bun.
4. Using a small knife, make 2 slits on 2 top bun halves and insert the ears.
5. Using scissors, cut 2 circles for the tiger's eyes, 1 oval and 1 line for the nose, and 7 large strips for the stripes from seaweed.
6. Cut 2 curved lines for the koala's eyes and a large oval for the nose from seaweed.
7. Butter 2 bottom halves of the buns and top with lettuce and slices of tomato and cucumber, and sandwich filling, Cover with the top halves of the buns.
8. Using a pair of tweezers, place the features on the tiger and koala. Dab a little mayonnaise on the parts to secure them to the bun.
9. Using a toothpick, dab a little ketchup on each bun for the cheeks.
10. Complete the bento meal with side dishes such as checkered apples and fried breaded prawns.

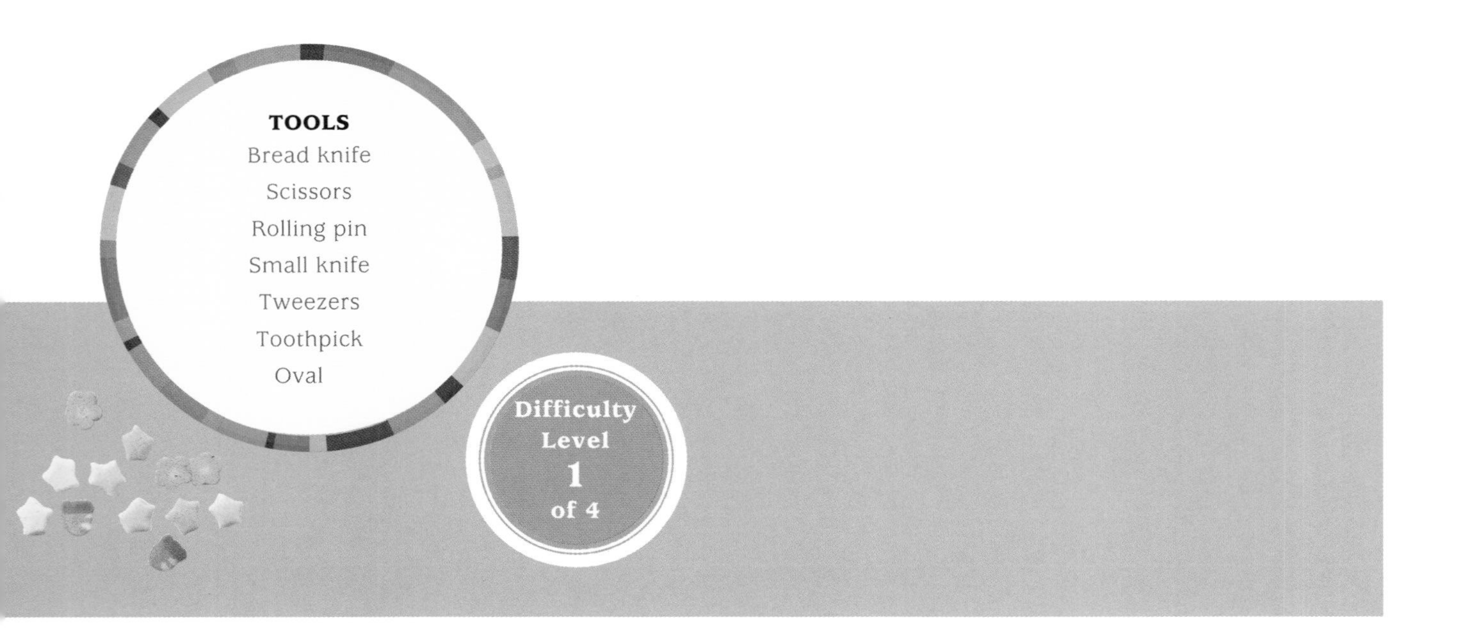

Ladybird Garden てんとう虫と蜂キャラ弁

Character Bento

1 pink quail egg (page 25)

1/2 seaweed sheet

A little mayonnaise

4 deep-fried pasta sticks, each about 2 cm

1 serving Japanese noodles

Lettuce

Carrot and sweet potato flowers (page 106)

Side Dishes

Grilled prawns

Lotus root meat patties

Vegetables of choice

Fresh fruit

1. Cut the quail egg lengthwise in half. Set aside.
2. Using scissors, cut 2 semicircles for the head, 2 strips for the wings and 8 circles for the spots from seaweed.
3. Using a pair of tweezers, place the features on the ladybirds, using some mayonnaise to help the parts stick to the egg.
4. Using a toothpick, pierce the top of the ladybirds' heads and insert the pasta sticks for the antenna.
5. Place the noodles and lettuce in the bento box and arrange the ladybirds on top. Decorate with the carrot and sweet potato flowers.
6. Complete the bento meal with side dishes such as grilled prawns, lotus root meat patties, vegetables of choice and fresh fruit. Add bento picks to enhance the theme, if desired.

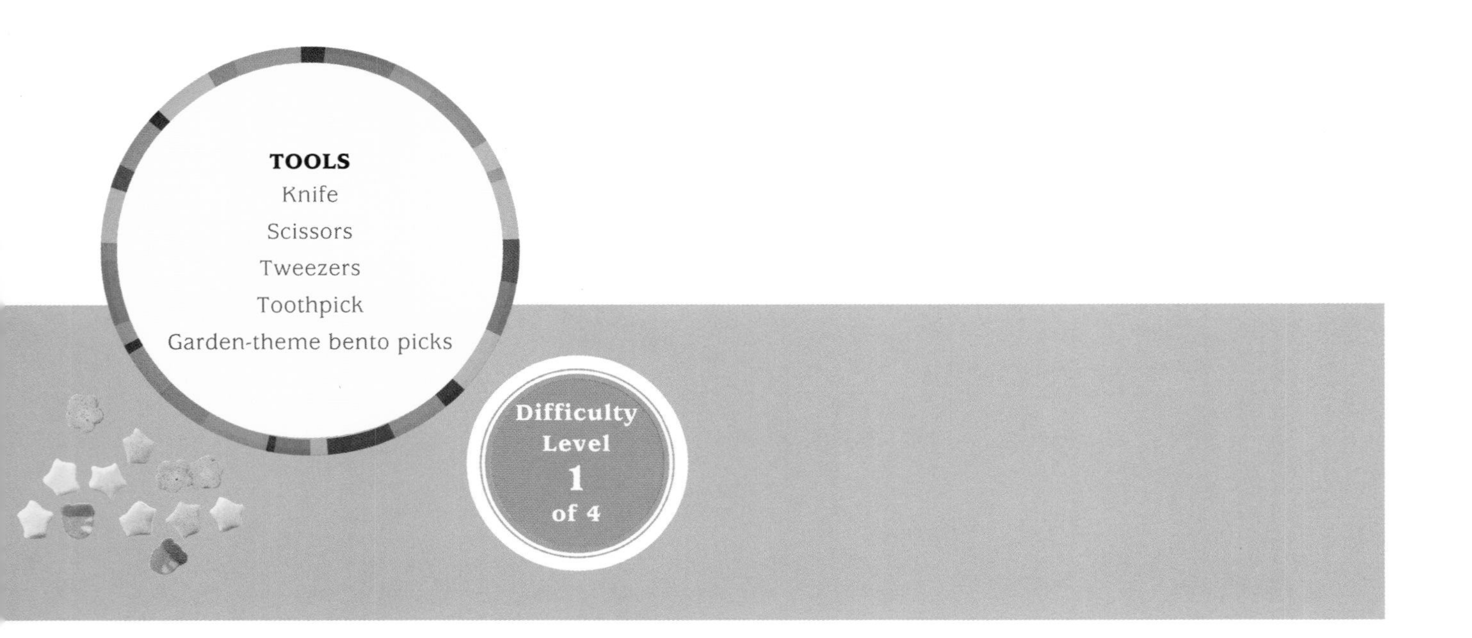

Little Red Riding Hood 96

Snow White 98

Three Little Pigs 100

Cinderella 102

Alice in Wonderland 104

Little Red Riding Hood 赤ずきんちゃんのキャラ弁

Character Bento

1/2 red egg sheet (page 26)

1/4 slice chicken ham

1/2 brown egg sheet (page 26)

1/2 seaweed sheet

Lettuce

2 slices French toast

A little mayonnaise

A little crabstick (*kani kamaboko*)

A few broccoli florets, boiled

Side Dishes

Potato salad with raisins and almonds

Fresh fruit

1. Trace the drawing of Little Red Riding Hood and the wolf (page 112) on a sheet of baking paper. Trace the parts (body, head, clothes and hair) separately as you will need to cut the different layers (page 29).
2. Using a pair of scissors, cut out the sections.
3. Place Red Riding Hood's body cut-out on the red egg sheet and cut using a precise cutting knife.
4. Place Red Riding Hood's head cut-out on the chicken ham and cut using a precise cutting knife.
5. Place the wolf's body cut-out on the brown egg sheet and cut using a precise cutting knife.
6. Using a pair of scissors, cut 2 semicircles for Red Riding Hood's hair, 2 small triangles for the wolf's inner ears and an oval for his nose from seaweed.
7. Using seaweed punches, cut Red Riding Hood's eyes and mouth and the wolf's eyes and mouth from seaweed
8. Line the bento box with lettuce and place the French toast in the box. Using tweezers, assemble Red Riding Hood and the wolf on the French toast. Dab a little mayonnaise on the ingredients to secure the layers.
9. Cut a red strip from the crabstick and make a tiny ribbon. Place it on Red Riding Hood's coat.
10. Arrange some broccoli florets on the French toast.
11. Complete the bento meal with sides dishes such as potato salad and fresh fruit.

TOOLS

Baking/parchment paper

Pencil

Precise cutting knife

Cutting board

Scissors

Seaweed punch

Tweezers

Difficulty Level 3 of 4

Snow White 白雪姫のキャラ弁

Character Bento

100–120 g cooked Japanese short-grain rice (page 20)

$^{1}/_{2}$–1 tsp teriyaki sauce

1 seaweed sheet

1 crabstick (*kani kamaboko*)

2 pasta sticks, each about 2 cm

Lettuce

2 tomato apples (page 111)

Side Dishes

Ginger-meat stir-fry (*shiogayaki*)

Vegetables of choice

1. Mix the rice evenly with the teriyaki sauce.
2. Using cling wrap, shape about $^{1}/_{2}$ tsp rice into an oblong for Snow White's arm. Shape about 1 tsp rice into a ball for Snow White's hair bun. Make two of these. Shape the remaining rice into a ball for Snow White's head.
3. Using a pair of scissors, cut out a wide inverted V for Snow White's fringe from one end of the sheet of seaweed, then cut the other side into a curve. Place it on the large rice ball and cut slits around the curved side of the seaweed, so it sits nicely around the rice ball for Snow White's hair (page 22). Cover with cling wrap. Set aside.
4. Cut 2 circles large enough to wrap around the hair buns from the seaweed. Cut slits around the sides and wrap the seaweed around the balls. Cover with cling wrap and set aside.
5. Using a pair of scissors, cut 2 circles for the eyes and a curved line for the mouth from seaweed.
6. Using a knife, make a slit along the side of the crabstick. Peel open and tear away the white layer, leaving only the red. Cut 4 red strips from the crabstick. Place 2 strips around Snow White's head for her hairband. Fold the other 2 strips into a ribbon and secure to the head with a pasta stick.
7. Line the bento box with lettuce and assemble Snow White in the box. Stick the hair buns to the head using pasta sticks. Using a pair of tweezers, place the features on the face. Place the tomato apples by the arm.
8. Complete the bento meal with side dishes such as ginger-meat stir-fry and vegetables of choice.
9. Add butterfly bento picks to enhance the theme, if desired.

TOOLS

Cling wrap

Scissors

Knife

Tweezers

Butterfly bento picks

Difficulty Level 2 of 4

Three Little Pigs 三匹の子豚のキャラ弁

Character Bento

120 g cooked Japanese short-grain rice (page 20)

1–1 1/2 tsp sushi seasoning mix

1 fried tofu pocket (*aburaage*)

1 slice ham

1/2 seaweed sheet

Lettuce

A little mayonnaise

Side Dishes

Grilled squid

Crabsticks (*kani kamaboko*)

Vegetables of choice

1. Mix the rice evenly with the sushi seasoning mix until the rice is pink in colour.
2. Divide the rice into 5 portions. Using cling wrap, shape 3 portions into balls for the pigs. Cover with cling wrap and set aside.
3. Peel open the fried tofu pocket and fill it with the remaining 2 portions of rice. Shape it into a rough oblong for the wolf's head.
4. Using a pair of scissors, cut a corner from the loose end of the tofu pocket for the wolf's ear. Wrap and tuck in the open end of the filled tofu pocket. Place the small triangle at the top corner for the ear.
5. Using a pair of scissors, cut 6 small triangles for the pig's ears from ham.
6. Using an oval cutter, cut 3 ovals for the pig's noses from ham. Using a small straw, cut out 2 holes for the nostrils from each oval.
7. Using a sakura petal cutter, cut 6 shapes for the pigs' trotters.
8. Using a seaweed punch, cut 3 pairs of eyes for the pigs from seaweed.
9. Using a pair of scissors, cut a thick jagged line for the wolf's mouth, a semicircle for the eye, a strip for the eyebrow and an oval for the nose from seaweed.
10. Line the bento box with lettuce and assemble the pigs and wolf in the box. Using a pair of tweezers, place the features on the characters. Dab a little mayonnaise on the ingredients to secure the layers.
11. Complete the bento meal with side dishes such as grilled squid, crabsticks and vegetables of choice.
12. Decorate with bento picks to enhance the theme, if desired.

TOOLS

Cling wrap

Scissors

Oval cutter

Small straw

Sakura petal cutter

Seaweed punch

Tweezers

Bento picks

Difficulty Level 1 of 4

Cinderella シンデレラのキャラ弁

Character Bento

100 g cooked Japanese short-grain rice (page 20)

1/2 tsp teriyaki sauce

Japanese yellow udon noodles, boiled

1 pasta stick, about 2 cm

1/4 seaweed sheet

A little ham

Side Dishes

Grilled cod

Bolognese sauce with deco pasta

Vegetables of choice

1. Mix the rice evenly with the teriyaki sauce.
2. Using cling wrap, shape Cinderella's hands, using about 1/2 tsp rice for each hand. Shape 1 tsp rice into a small ball for her hair bun. Shape the remaining rice for her head.
3. Wrap the yellow udon noodles around the head to create hair. Place Cinderella's head into the bento box.
4. Wrap the smaller rice ball for the hair bun with yellow udon noodles and attach it to the head with a pasta stick. Add a princess tiara bento pick.
5. Using scissors, cut 2 ovals for the eyes, 4 lines for the eyelashes and a curved line for the mouth from seaweed.
6. Using a small heart cutter, cut out 2 hearts from ham for the cheeks.
7. Using a pair of tweezers, place the features on the face. Assemble the hands and stick a star bento pick into one hand.
8. Complete the bento meal with sides dishes such as grilled cod, Bolognese sauce with deco pasta and vegetables of choice.
9. Decorate with a glass shoe bento pick if desired.

TOOLS

Cling wrap
Tiara bento pick
Small heart cutter
Scissors
Tweezers
Star bento pick
Glass shoe bento pick

Difficulty Level 3 of 4

Alice in Wonderland 不思議の国のアリスのキャラ弁

Character Bento

1 seaweed sheet

1 oblate sheet

Yellow, orange, blue, green, brown and red food colouring

Water, as needed

170–180 g cooked Japanese short-grain rice (page 20)

Hamburger patty clock (page 109)

Side Dishes

Deco sausages (page 109)

Meat croquettes

Vegetables of choice

1. Trace or make 2 copies of the Alice in Wonderland design on page 113.
2. Follow the steps on page 29 to cut out, paste and colour the design.
3. Spoon the rice into the bento box. Place the design on the rice.
4. Complete the bento meal with meat croquettes and vegetables of choice. Decorate with the hamburger patty clock.

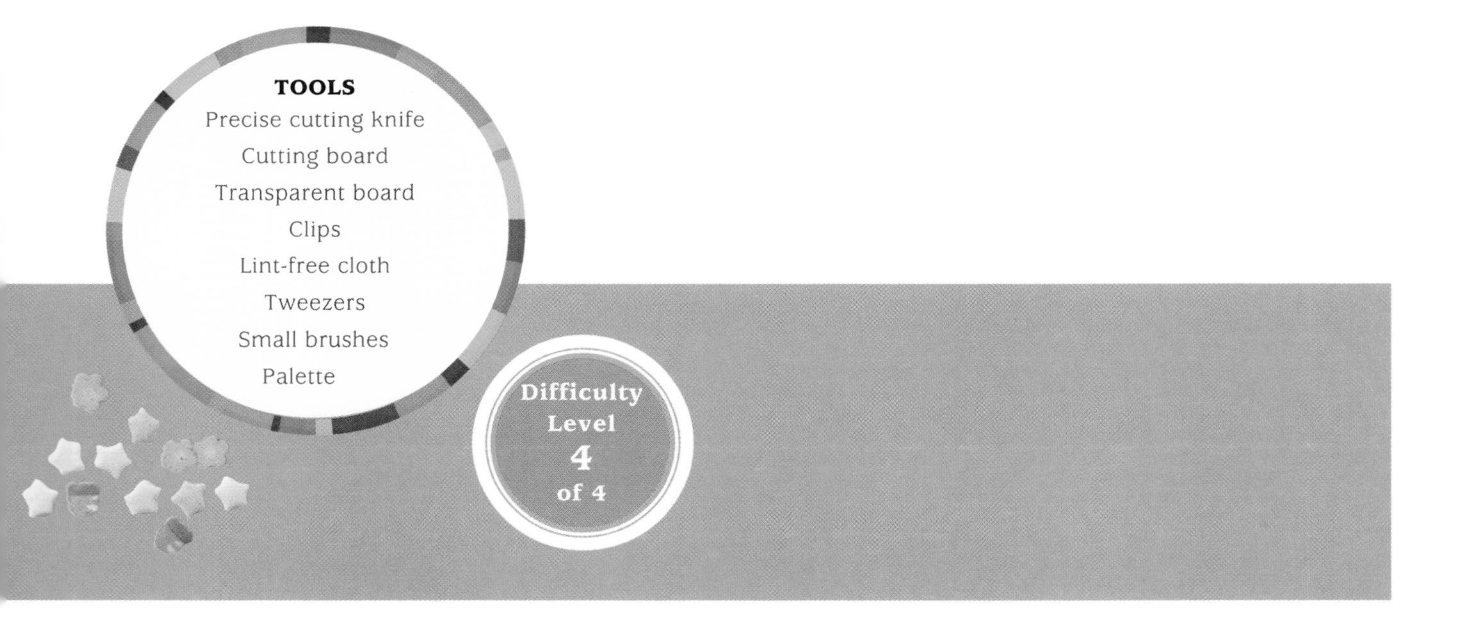

Bento Decorative Items

Ham Sakura Flowers

Thickly sliced ham

- Using a sakura flower cutter, cut sakura flowers from the ham.
- Using a small sharp knife, make shallow cuts to define each petal. To create a 3D look, hold the knife at an angle and make diagonal cuts.

Carrot and Sweet Potato Flowers

Carrot

Sweet potato

- Cut the carrot/sweet potato into slices approximately 0.5-cm thick.
- Using a 5-petal flower cutter, cut out flower shapes from the carrot/sweet potato slices.
- Using a small sharp knife, make shallow cuts to define each petal. To create a 3D look, hold the knife at an angle and make diagonal cuts.

Ham Flower

Thinly sliced ham

Pasta stick

- Fold the ham in half. On the folded end, make a series of parallel cuts using a knife. The cuts should be at close, regular intervals, and about 1.5-cm long.
- Roll the ham up tightly and secure with a short length of pasta stick.
- Using a knife, trim off the excess ham at the bottom so the ham flower can stand upright.

Egg Sheet Graduation Scroll

Yellow egg sheet (page 26)

Crabstick (*kani kamaboko*)

Pasta stick

- Using a pair of scissors, cut a small rectangle from the yellow egg sheet.
- Using a knife, make a slit along the side of the crabstick. Peel open and cut 2 thin strips from the red layer.
- Roll up the egg sheet to create the scroll, then wrap a strip of crabstick around it. Trim the crabstick and secure it to the egg sheet with a short length of pasta stick.
- Tie the other strip of crabstick into a knot and place it on the scroll.

Tamago Cake

2 eggs

30 ml Japanese soup stock (dashi)

1 tsp Japanese light soy sauce

1 tsp sugar

Ham

Cake-theme bento picks

- Prepare Japanese egg roll. Beat eggs in a bowl. Add stock, soy sauce and sugar and mix lightly.
- Lightly oil a frying pan. Pour a thin layer of egg mixture into the pan. Cook over low heat. When lightly set, roll egg into a log and push to one side of the pan.
- Add another layer of egg mixture and cook until lightly set. Roll the first layer into the second layer. Repeat to cook and roll until egg is used up. There should be a minimum of 3 layers.
- Shape egg roll using a sushi mat, then trim and cut into 2 slices, each about 1.5-cm thick. Trim and cut the ham to match the shape of the egg roll. Sandwich the ham between the slices of egg roll.
- Secure the layers with cake-theme bento picks to complete the cake.

Tamago Gift Box

Japanese egg roll (*tamagoyaki*)

Crabstick (*kani kamaboko*)

- Prepare egg roll. (See *tamago* cake.)
- Trim and cut the egg roll into a small cube.
- Using a knife, make a slit along the side of the crabstick. Peel open and cut 2 thin strips from the red layer.
- Wrap the strips of crabstick around the egg roll cube. Secure at the bottom with a short length of pasta stick and at the top with a bento pick to complete the gift box.

Sausage Egg Sunflower

Sausage

Yellow egg sheet (page 26)

Pasta stick

- Using a knife, trim the ends of the sausage, then cut into a 3-cm length. Make small right angled cuts on one end of the sausage.
- Boil a pot of water and add the sausage. Cook until the cut end opens up and the design is obvious. Drain and set aside.
- Fold the egg sheet in half. On the folded end, make a series of parallel cuts using a knife. The cuts should be at close, regular intervals, and about 1.5-cm long.
- Roll the egg sheet up tightly around the sausage, keeping the decorative ends of the egg sheet and sausage on the same side. Secure with a short length of pasta stick.
- Using a knife, trim off the excess egg sheet at the bottom so the sunflower can stand upright.

Sausage Crab

Red sausage

Seaweed

Egg white sheet (page 26)

Pasta stick

- Cut the sausage lengthwise in half. Make 3 short slits on either end of the sausage to create the legs. Make a small X at the centre to create the crab's body.
- Boil a pot of water and add the sausage. Cook until the cut ends open up and the design is obvious.
- Using the other half of the sausage, cut 2 pieces for the crab's claws. Attach to the crab body using short lengths of pasta stick.
- Using a straw, cut 2 circles for the eyes from the egg white sheet. Using a seaweed cutter, cut a shape for the eyes from seaweed to complete the eyes.
- Place the eyes on the crab. Use a little mayonnaise to help the seaweed stick to the egg sheet, if necessary.

Sausage Acorn

Cocktail sausage

Shimeiji mushroom, cooked

Deep-fried pasta stick

- Trim one end of the cocktail sausage. This will be the top of the acorn.
- Trim the stalk of the shimeiji mushroom, leaving only the cap.
- Place the mushroom cap over the cut end of the sausage. Secure with a deep fried pasta stick to create the stalk and complete the acorn.

Deco Sausage

Mini sausage

- Cut both ends of the sausage.
- Using a small star cutter, make a cut in the centre on one end of the sausage .
- From the cut shape, make cuts from the centre outwards.
- Boil a pot of water and add the sausage. Cook until the cut end opens up and the design is obvious. Drain.

Seaweed Bat

Seaweed

Ham

- Using a pair of scissors, cut the head, wings and body of the bat separately from seaweed.
- Assemble the seaweed parts on the ham.
- Using a precise cutting knife, cut the ham following the shape of the bat.

Hamburger Patty Clock

Minced meat patty

Egg white sheet (page 26)

Seaweed

Crabstick (*kani kamaboko*)

Pasta stick

Bento pick

- Using a pair of scissors, cut a circle slightly smaller than the meat patty for the clock face from the egg white sheet.
- Using a pair of scissors, cut small strips for the Roman numerals and clock hands.
- Using a knife, make a slit along the side of the crabstick. Peel open. Using a small heart cutter, cut 2 heart shapes for the clock hands from the red layer.
- Assemble the parts. Secure the egg white sheet to the meat patty using short lengths of pasta stick. Use a little mayonnaise to help the seaweed stick to the egg sheet, if necessary.
- Insert a bento pick into the clock.

Cucumber Tortoise

Japanese cucumber

Egg white sheet (page 26)

Seaweed

- Trim the ends of the cucumber and cut a length about 5-cm long. Cut it lengthwise in half, then cut away the light green flesh, leaving a thin layer under the dark green skin. Flatten the cucumber gently.
- Using an oval cutter, cut out an oval from the cucumber. Using a small sharp knife, make criss-cross cuts diagonally on the skin to create the pattern on the tortoise's shell.
- Cut a slice of cucumber about 0.5-cm thick. Using a small oval cutter, cut 4 ovals for the legs. Using a medium oval cutter, cut another oval for the head. Trim with a knife to shape the head if necessary. Using a knife, cut a small triangle for the tail.
- Using a straw, cut 2 circles for the eyes from the egg white sheet. Using a seaweed cutter, cut 2 curved lines from seaweed to complete the eyes.
- Assemble the parts. Use a little mayonnaise to help the seaweed stick to the egg sheet, if necessary.

Green Bean Bamboo

Green beans

- Using a knife, trim the green beans, then make cuts at 2-cm intervals down the length to create the nodes. Leave 1 green bean uncut.
- Boil a pot of water and add the green beans. Cook for 2–3 minutes, then remove and place in a bowl of cold water. This will help the green beans retain their bright green colour.
- Holding the knife at an angle, cut the uncut green bean into diagonal slices.
- Arrange the diagonal slices with the green beans to complete the bamboo.

Checked Apples

Red apple

Green apple

Lemon juice

- Cut each apple into quarters. Remove the core and seeds.
- Spray the cut apples with lemon juice to prevent discolouration.
- Using a knife, make shallow longitudinal cuts on the skin of the apples, then repeat to make cuts across the apple skin to form small squares.
- Remove alternate squares of skin from the apple to create the checked pattern. While cutting, spray the apple with some lemon juice to prevent discolouration.

Tomato Rose

Ripe and firm tomato

- Using a small sharp knife, start slicing the skin of the tomato from the base of the tomato.
- Cut a strip from the base, then continue cutting around the tomato, keeping the strip about 2.5-cm wide.
- Starting from the top end of the strip, roll the length of tomato skin around itself, with the skin side facing out. You should see the shape of the rose forming.
- Continue rolling until you reach the end. Tuck the base under the rose.

Tomato Apple

Cherry tomato

Mini asparagus

Cheese

Black sesame seeds

- Halve the cherry tomato.
- Using a round cutter smaller than the diameter of the tomato, cut a circle for the core of the apple from the cheese. Halve it to make 2 semicircles.
- Place the cheese on the the cut side of the tomato. Using a pair of tweezers, place 3 black sesame seeds on each slice of cheese to resemble the core of the apple.
- Boil the asparagus until tender, then slice to resemble the apple's stem.
- Using a toothpick, pierce the top of the tomato and insert the asparagus into the slit to complete the apple.

Quail Egg Ghost

Quail egg

Seaweed

Ham

- Place the quail egg in a saucepan filled with water. Bring to the boil and cook for 6–7 minutes.
- Remove the hard-boiled egg and peel.
- While the egg is still warm, gently mould it with your hands so it is pointed at one end. Set aside.
- Using a seaweed punch, cut 2 ovals for the eyes and 2 curved lines for the eyebrows from seaweed.
- Using a precise cutting knife or oval cutter, cut 2 curved pieces for the mouth from ham.
- Using a pair of tweezers, place the features on the quail egg. Use a little mayonnaise to help the seaweed stick to the egg, if necessary.

Character Templates

Choose a character template and trace it on baking paper according to the instructions on page 29. These designs are drawn to scale and can be used as they are.

Autumn Magic
(page 50)

Little Red Riding Hood
(page 96)

Marital Bliss
(page 60)

Alice in Wonderland
(page 104)

Mermaid
(page 29)

Panda
(page 30)

Stockists

Here is a list of retailers where I get many of my bento supplies from. Have fun shopping!

Bento&co
www.bentoandco.com

BentoUSA
www.BentoUSA.com

Isetan
www.isetan.com.sg

Meidi-ya
www.meidi-ya.com.sg

Weights & Measures

Quantities for this book are given in Metric and American (spoon) measures. Standard spoon and cup measurements used are: 1 tsp = 5 ml, 1 Tbsp = 15 ml, 1 cup = 250 ml. All measures are level unless otherwise stated.

LIQUID AND VOLUME MEASURES

Metric	Imperial	American
5 ml	1/6 fl oz	1 teaspoon
10 ml	1/3 fl oz	1 dessertspoon
15 ml	1/2 fl oz	1 tablespoon
60 ml	2 fl oz	1/4 cup (4 tablespoons)
85 ml	2 1/2 fl oz	1/3 cup
90 ml	3 fl oz	3/8 cup (6 tablespoons)
125 ml	4 fl oz	1/2 cup
180 ml	6 fl oz	3/4 cup
250 ml	8 fl oz	1 cup
300 ml	10 fl oz (1/2 pint)	1 1/4 cups
375 ml	12 fl oz	1 1/2 cups
435 ml	14 fl oz	1 3/4 cups
500 ml	16 fl oz	2 cups
625 ml	20 fl oz (1 pint)	2 1/2 cups
750 ml	24 fl oz (1 1/5 pints)	3 cups
1 litre	32 fl oz (1 3/5 pints)	4 cups
1.25 litres	40 fl oz (2 pints)	5 cups
1.5 litres	48 fl oz (2 2/5 pints)	6 cups
2.5 litres	80 fl oz (4 pints)	10 cups

DRY MEASURES

Metric	Imperial
30 grams	1 ounce
45 grams	1 1/2 ounces
55 grams	2 ounces
70 grams	2 1/2 ounces
85 grams	3 ounces
100 grams	3 1/2 ounces
110 grams	4 ounces
125 grams	4 1/2 ounces
140 grams	5 ounces
280 grams	10 ounces
450 grams	16 ounces (1 pound)
500 grams	1 pound, 1 1/2 ounces
700 grams	1 1/2 pounds
800 grams	1 3/4 pounds
1 kilogram	2 pounds, 3 ounces
1.5 kilograms	3 pounds, 4 1/2 ounces
2 kilograms	4 pounds, 6 ounces

OVEN TEMPERATURE

	°C	°F	Gas Regulo
Very slow	120	250	1
Slow	150	300	2
Moderately slow	160	325	3
Moderate	180	350	4
Moderately hot	190/200	370/400	5/6
Hot	210/220	410/440	6/7
Very hot	230	450	8
Super hot	250/290	475/550	9/10

LENGTH

Metric	Imperial
0.5 cm	1/4 inch
1 cm	1/2 inch
1.5 cm	3/4 inch
2.5 cm	1 inch